HOME GROWN

HOME GROWN

ADVENTURES *in* PARENTING *off the* BEATEN PATH,
UNSCHOOLING, *and* RECONNECTING *with*
the NATURAL WORLD

Ben Hewitt

Roost Books
Boston & London 2014

Roost Books
An imprint of Shambhala Publications, Inc.
Horticultural Hall
300 Massachusetts Avenue
Boston, Massachusetts 02115
Roostbooks.com

9 8 7 6 5 4 3 2 1

First Edition
Printed in the United States of America

⊗This edition is printed on acid-free paper that meets the American National
Standards Institute z39.48 Standard.
♻This book is printed on 30% postconsumer recycled paper.
For more information please visit www.shambhala.com.

Distributed in the United States by Penguin Random House LLC
and in Canada by Random House of Canada Ltd

Designed by Daniel Urban-Brown

LIBRARY OF CONGRESS CATALOGING-IN-PUBLICATION DATA
Hewitt, Ben, 1971–
Home grown: adventures in parenting off the beaten path, unschooling, and
reconnecting with the natural world / Ben Hewitt.
pages cm
Includes bibliographical references and index.
ISBN 978-1-61180-169-9 (paperback)
1. Home schooling. 2. Non-formal education. 3. Education—Parent participation.
4. Parenting. 5. Nature study. 6. Outdoor education. 7. Experiential learning. 8.
Sustainable living. I. Title.
LC40.H56 2014
371.04'2—dc23
2013050554

Contents

Acknowledgments

More so than anything else I've written, this book belongs to my family, and my gratitude to them is boundless. Without my sons, ever-generous in the sharing of their wisdom and delight, it could not have happened. Without Penny, whose commitment to our family and the land endlessly inspires me, it could not have happened. Generosity and commitment are acts born of love, and I am humbled to be the recipient of such gifts. I only hope I can return at least a fraction of what I receive.

I also wish to thank my editor, Rochelle Bourgault. Only Rochelle truly knows how much this book has evolved from its early drafts, and if I can ask just one more favor of her, it'd be to keep that little secret between us. In return, I will loudly and repeatedly let it be known that without Rochelle's guidance, insight, and enduring patience, this book would be merely a shadow of what it has become.

Finally, thanks to my friend Janet MacLeod for generously contributing the art that adds so much to these pages.

Prologue:
The World at Hand

FIN HAS MADE A BOW. It is gorgeous, long and slender and burnished, its surface silken to the touch. So many hours with his hands on that one length of wood, carving and sanding, or merely for the pleasure of feeling, and it occurs to me that he knows this piece of wood in a way that no one else ever will. In some unspoken way, in a language older than words, he has come to understand its intentions, even as he has communicated his.

"Watch this," he says. He pulls back the string and the bow bends. It seems to me as if it should not be able to bend so far without breaking. He slowly releases the tension. "It's my best one yet."

How many bows has Fin made? Thirty? Forty? Certainly more than I can say, more than I've kept track of. The first ones of simple sticks, short whips of red maple or yellow birch, notches carved into each end where a string could be wound. The arrows were sticks, too, straight-ish but not straight, capable of a dozen feet of wobbly, slow-motion flight, like a fledgling leaving the nest for the first time. And now, this: a bow hewn of black locust, not merely made but crafted, exactingly tillered for even draw, micrometers of wood fiber shaved at a time until the top and bottom halves flex in perfect symmetry. It is the evolved embodiment of all its predecessors, some long ago broken and fed to the fire, more simply forgotten, abandoned in a corner of the barn or basement. I stumble across them but cannot quite bring myself to discard them. They are evidence of my older son's studied persistence, an immersion into whatever wild corners of his heart and mind have given rise to this passion. For that reason alone, I leave them where they lie.

My children do not attend school, and often when people hear of this, I am asked how my sons (Fin and his younger brother, named Rye) learn, or how we teach them, or some combination of the two. And I struggle with my reply, probably because I feel as if the answer being sought will never satisfy the assumptions inherent in the question: that children must be taught to learn. That learning is something that happens primarily in isolation from other aspects of their lives. That teaching is best left to specialists. But of course children needn't be taught how to learn; they just do. It is as natural and obvious as breathing, as necessary to their spiritual, emotional, and intellectual beings as food is to their physical manifestations.

Like so much of what my sons know and do, Fin did not learn how to craft a bow because someone told him he should learn to craft a bow. He learned because he had no choice but to learn, because his innate curiosity and desire to learn simply could not be overcome. In the same way that you cannot stop children from learning to walk, or to talk, you cannot stop them from learning anything they set their minds to.

That is why I say that learning is my children's nature, just as it is every child's nature. I am reminded of this when I see Fin bent over his bow, rubbing it again with an oiled cloth, so intent on the task that his world has folded in on itself. What does each pass along the bow's spine teach him? What does it tell him about the bow, about the tree, about the process? About himself and his place in the world? And I am reminded of this on late-winter mornings when I look out the window above the kitchen sink, the stars still visible in the brightening sky, and I see Rye tromping through the snow, laden with the implements of tapping sugar maple trees in preparation for the season's first sap run: a cordless drill, a hammer, a small bucketful of taps. Like his older brother, my second child is drawn to tasks that involve the hands and that yield something tangible.

In these moments, it often occurs to me that while we are so-cialized to believe that our children's lives should be constantly ex-panding into new horizons and opportunities, could it be that we are ignoring (or simply ignorant of) the value of having their world contract? Perhaps we should pause to stem the distractions of this big and wondrous world, so full of possibilities and choice that no matter how determined we are, we cannot expose them to more than the smallest fraction of its offerings. Maybe we could start to show them the richness of experience that waits directly outside our front doors, in our neighborhoods and communities—in our imaginations, even. This is the dream I can't quite kick, although I sometimes wonder if it's not a selfish one: my boys will not chase the infinite possibilities of the world at large, but wherever they may be, they will instead continue to find fulfillment in the world at hand.

A few days after Fin rubbed the final coat of oil into that slen-der stave of bow wood, I watched from my home-office window as he carried it across the long expanse of our meadow. It was a cool morning, and a soft rain hung in the air. My son walked quickly, and I did not know where he was going, or what purpose drew him, and for the briefest of moments I was visited by the sense that it was not he who was taking the bow with him, but rather the op-posite. The bow was leading him. I imagined pushing away from my desk, running down the stairs and out the door, calling after my boy, "Wait! Wait! I want to come!"

But I did not, and I knew it was right that I did not, and so I merely watched as he disappeared into a dense stand of fir.

Introduction

As I MENTIONED briefly in the prologue, my sons do not attend school. The manner and content of their learning outside the boundaries of the formal education system is much of what this book is about, but because this manner and content cannot be separated from so many other aspects of our life on this Vermont hillside, the stories that follow are not at first glance solely about learning, at least not in the manner we have come to think of learning in this culture. What's more, the stories I share in the following pages are not merely about my children's education but also about my wife, Penny's, and mine and our evolving understanding of how to make our way in this world, informed by our connection to this very piece of land and our work upon it. They are not merely stories about all we are learning but also about all we are *unlearning,* and about our imperfect quest to inhabit a balanced place that allows us to remain part of the broader world while also living in a way that is true to our values and vision. In a sense, for us this has been the easy part. I have found that the harder part is determining how to conduct our lives in a manner that honors these values and this vision, even as we are continually confronted with evidence that such a quest is impractical, if not downright naive.

It is the longing for connection to nature and place, along with our belief that such connections are essential to the development of human intellect and spirit that largely informs our decision to keep

4

Fin and Rye out of school. Every hour a child spends in school is an hour he or she is not free to develop these connections outside the microcosm of the classroom. And those hours are not insignificant: Recently, Penny and I calculated the amount of time our sons would already have spent in a classroom if such were their destiny. For Fin, who would likely have already spent six of his twelve years in school, it added up to approximately eight thousand hours, not including homework and commuting time. For Rye, it'd be about half that. When we tacked on the thirty-four hours of television the average American child watches each and every week (we do not own a television), we arrived at the stunning conclusion that in just the past half-dozen years, our elder son would have spent nearly nineteen thousand hours either in school or in front of a TV screen. Assuming he spends fourteen hours of each day awake, that's more than three-and-a-half *years* of his waking life, out of only the past six. None of these calculations even includes the plethora of digital devices that command an ever-increasing portion of our children's attention.

Is there really anything my sons might learn in school—to say nothing of what is learned in front of the television or peering into a smartphone—that is worth giving up so much of their lives for? Already I have seen how quickly and willingly they master the rote information necessary to make their way in this world, the reading, writing, spelling, and basic math every person needs to communicate with their community. Having witnessed my sons' capacity to assimilate these skills without interference from an accredited educator or even from Penny or myself, I can report with confidence that formal instruction in these subjects is unnecessary. And while I am not prepared to say there is nothing else of value my boys might learn in those thousands upon thousands of confined classroom hours, I am certain there are more beneficial ways for them to pass their time. I have seen that what they learn when they are granted freedom of exploration and expression, and when they are given opportunity to pursue their true passions without fear of judgment or failure, is much more than a formal education can offer.

Penny and I do not believe that school is a place of ill intentions. Indeed, it is almost certainly the opposite. But the problems with the way the vast majority of schools are currently structured are inherent in that structure. They are built into the system, with its grading and confinement and stratified social order. In fact, they are so much a part of the way children are educated that even the many well-intentioned and devoted people working within this system cannot overcome the flaws intrinsic to structured compulsory learning. These decent and caring people cannot give my sons back all those thousands of hours. They can do relatively little to help them know and feel and love the very place where they live, or their community beyond their immediate peer groups. They are unlikely to bring my children closer to the plants and creatures of the land, or the land itself. They will not follow them to a century-old maple tree and sit quietly at its base and wonder with them if perhaps they really can feel the tree breathing.

These are things we wish to provide for our children and, it must be said, for ourselves. These are the things that we believe will allow our sons and us to develop into full expressions of the people we can be. We have come to see our ability to live in this manner as the defining blessing of our time on this earth and the greatest measure of our wealth.

The stories in the following pages are rooted primarily in observation and experience. They are merely the findings of one person and one family. Still, I will occasionally support my layperson's perspective with opinions and data supplied by experts in the field. But even though I offer these findings as support for my positions, I hasten to remind you that just because someone—including myself—says something is so does not make it so for *you*. In other words, it is not so much my intention for this book to convince you of anything in particular but rather to share my family's journey toward gaining the confidence to trust in our own beliefs and innate wisdom with the hope that it may help you trust in *your* innate wisdom.

My intent is not to show you how perfect our life is, nor how we've mastered the fine art of educating and parenting in place, all of which would be a lie anyway. Our life is imperfect in no small part because *we* are imperfect people inhabiting an imperfect world. We have not mastered the fine art of educating and parenting any more than any other educator or parent has. Like our children, we are learning all the time, and I hope the only thing that can stop us from learning is death. All I can say for certain is that our lives, like yours, are full of joy and despair, struggle and triumph, certainty and uncertainty, and that our views continue to evolve with the passage of time.

In my own life, I am repeatedly struck by the truth that the more thoroughly I liberate myself from prevailing cultural assumptions— around education, wealth, ambition, and success, to name but a few— the more choice I actually have. The more *freedom* I have. In some regards, this is obvious, because if I'm not devoting my days to the accumulation of money and status, I am liberated to pursue other things. But the freedom I speak of is more than temporal; it is also a freedom of emotion and spirit, to know that happiness and fulfillment can be found in the smallest and simplest of places and things. I think of the austere dullness of a November day, the gradations of color reduced to slim subtleties, beauty defined as much by what is absent as by what is present. I think of the way I'm so often caught off guard by some small, commonplace moment: the sight of our pet Muscovy duck, Web, waddling across the pasture; or seeing Fin and Rye moving over the land together on their way to or from the woods. From the way their heads are tipped just the slightest bit toward one another, I know they are talking. Sometimes, I cannot even identify a trigger, like when I am walking down the farm road and I am suddenly swept by a sense of knowing my place. Not just in the here and now, but in the grand, infinite scheme of things and forces far beyond my capacity to even imagine.

What I gain from these moments—the quick bloom of warmth they bring, the quiet sense of knowing that there is nothing else I need—cannot be readily measured, and because it cannot be measured, it cannot be traded. It is my own wealth. It is unique to me and therefore it is secure.

It is at once liberating, daunting, exciting, and, it must be said, occasionally frightening to realize the extent to which my world is in my hands. I am freer than I was told as a child; I am freer than I was led to believe.

This is my true power, and it is not the false power of that which can be bought or traded or accumulated. What I do with my life—how I raise my children, how I engage with others and with the natural world, and how I pass my time—is an expression of my belief in what is possible. It is an expression of my vision for the world I wish to inhabit, and for the world I wish for my children to inhabit.

It is a huge honor to share my vision for this world—or parts of it, at least—with you. I am grateful for the opportunity, and I am grateful for the gift of your time and attention.

Moving Cows

In the early mornings of summer, before it is fully light, I walk the rutted farm road to the lower pasture, where I'll move the cows into a fresh paddock for the day's grazing. The road curves past the greenhouse where the slowly ripening tomato crop hangs from weary vines, then past the sawmill with the unfinished frame of its roof looming over me like an admonishment, one of those tasks that never seems to rise high enough on the ever-shifting list of priorities to earn our attention. Past the currant bushes Rye planted the summer before, hauling fieldstones in his wagon to fashion a protective border around them. He'd been afraid I'd crush them with the tractor, and how could I blame him? There was precedent for such concern. Past the chicken coop, where our rooster, Blood, crows lustily, tending to his harem in the manner of all roosters throughout millennia.

Of all the daily chores I perform on this small farm, moving the cows feels most like a dance, its movements rehearsed and refined over thousands of mornings. My partners lumber and shuffle as they position themselves by the corner of the fence they know will be first to drop. When it does, they move with uncharacteristic zeal, heads bent to the dew-wet grass rising above their knees like ocean surf. Cows are not terribly ambitious creatures—this is much of what I love about them—but a paddock of lush fodder awakens something primal in them. I suspect it's not dissimilar to the thing that awakens in me when Penny pulls a batch of cookies from the oven.

I love moving cows because I get to come back from moving cows, retracing my steps in the milky light of predawn. Often, I am returning at just the moment my family is emerging from the house, embarking on their respective chores, and I stop simply for the pleasure of the scene before me. Penny going to collect Apple for morning milking, striding down the cow path in that purposeful way of hers, the sun just beginning to illuminate the eastern horizon behind her. Rye walking toward the goat pen, the implements of his task dangling from his small hands: the pail of warm water for washing Flora's udder and his little quart milking jug. Behind him, Fin carrying a flake of hay and a bucket of water. For a moment, one of those fragments of time when everything seems to coalesce in a way that answers some unasked question, I know everything I need to know. I feel everything I need to feel.

I am just realizing, late learner that I am, the extent to which it is not just the sights, but also the smells, sounds, and tactile sensations of our little farm that add to my life. Past the tomato house, the thick scent of soil and sharp, strangely acrid-sweet smell of ripening fruit. Past the sawmill, and the smell of sawdust, like bread baking. At the sugar bush, the movement of the leaves, like someone whispering something in your ear that you can't quite make out, and with it the push of breeze across my face, maybe lifting off the pond or funneling down the pasture on a northward trajectory. Past the chickens, and the learned response of pleasure at the smell of their manure, knowing what it does for the tomatoes. Growing food is one of those rare undertakings with the capacity to alter your perceptions so completely that something that might once have seemed objectionable and even disgusting becomes beautiful as the elegance of its true purpose is revealed. Down by the cows, the distinctive smell of bovine—the warm, contented essence of their being.

In winter, there is a distinct shift. Instead, the air smells of hay as I feed the cows every morning and evening. At least once a day, one or more of the cows kindly tolerates me burying my face in their soft hides and simply breathing for a minute, one of the small, strange luxuries in my small, strange life. And fresh-cut wood: for the sawmill, fir and spruce and hemlock, and for the woodstove, maple and beech, birch and ash. Even the saw has a smell, the specific acridness of a two-stroke motor run hot and fast. Every morning, before anything else, the first hungry flame of the cookstove fire, and then the burned odor of coffee bubbling over onto the stovetop.

The older I get, the more I find myself sniffing the air, or reaching to run a hand across one of the animals' backs, or simply standing and listening to the ever-changing melody of our place. I did not used to do these things, or if I did, not so frequently and consciously, and I think this is because the more I have allowed myself to experience this place, the more I have come to appreciate it. And the more I come to appreciate it, the more I am able to experience it, to become immersed in it, to perceive myself as being what I truly am. Not master of my domain, but in truth little more than a thread woven into its fabric, merely one of the millions of small threads—some visible, but many more not—that comprise the whole.

1

The Reckoning

A BIT MORE THAN FOUR YEARS after we first walked the land we would eventually purchase, Penny and I became parents when our first son, Finlay, was born. (Rye was born nearly three years later).

Of all the things I have learned since becoming a parent (and sometimes, it feels as if this might be *everything* I've ever learned), perhaps the hardest to accept is that it is selfish and possibly even dangerous to desire particular outcomes for our children. This is in no small part because we cannot be masters of our children's fates, and to pretend otherwise is to engage in both delusion and hubris. This does not stop parents from trying, of course. We are forever attempting to engineer our children's lives, most often in ways we believe will deliver them to some predetermined future, and I often remind myself that whatever stories my sons choose to write with their lives are not mine to tell or even to imagine.

This is not to say that we are helpless to direct our children. Rather, it is an acknowledgment of the simple fact that our sons and daughters will *always* find ways to surprise us, and that often these surprises will thwart specific hopes we might have held on their behalf. In my experience, the more specific the hope, the more likely it will go unfulfilled. But of course I cannot fully stop myself from wanting on my boys' behalf. I am their father, after all. I am only human.

Of all the things I want for them, connection to place and a sense of knowing how they fit into this world usurps all others. I want this for them more than happiness, because I think mere happiness is a shallow elucidation of the human experience, and by itself is not a particularly sturdy emotional foundation upon which to build a fulfilling life. I want this for them more than success, at least insofar as our culture has come to define success as being a product of money and power and recognition. I want this for them more than physical vitality, because I believe that good health—and not just health of body, but also of emotion and spirit—is only possible when one feels connected to and secure in their place.

To be clear, this does not mean that my sons must remain on this land until the end of their physical lives; while the connection I'm talking about can surely be instilled by a particular place, this connection can also travel, because this connection is a bond that cannot be broken. It is permanent and unconditional, and it is impervious to distance or circumstance, much like the bond between siblings or parent and child. In this sense, it is not even a connection to a specific place; it is a connection to *oneself*. It is a sense of understanding how one fits into a great, vast world in which both beauty and tragedy can overwhelm.

I don't know precisely what this connection looks and feels like, in part because Penny and I are learning the shape of this connection alongside our sons. Like most children of our generation—indeed, like most children of our sons' generation—we did not grow up free to determine our place in the world. Like most children, we were *told* our place. We were not told this unkindly, nor without tremendous love. We were not told this overtly. Rather, we were unquestioningly expected to do as the majority of our childhood peers did, with little consideration given as to what was truly being asked of us and what the cost might be. Along with the vast majority of our peers, Penny and I passed the formative years of our respective childhoods in school, as students of what we were told we must learn. That there are other ways of learning was never considered. That there are other things to learn, many of which cannot be measured or graded or segregated by subject, was never discussed. That our prescribed educations might actually erode our self-confidence, rather than develop it, occurred to no one.

It is not difficult to understand why these things were not considered or discussed; it is not difficult to understand why it occurred to no one that passing the majority of our childhood in school might strip us of confidence. *Because the same thing happened to our parents.* To call into question the wisdom of convention requires a degree of self-assuredness that rarely survives the eroding impact of standardized, hierarchical education. Such questioning also places one in the uncomfortable position of cutting against the cultural grain, of being perceived as arrogant, eccentric, perhaps even dangerous, and few parents—including Penny and myself—wish to be perceived in this manner.

I realize there is nothing I can do to guarantee that Fin and Rye will develop the connection I speak of. The uncomfortable truth lurking in every parent's heart—including mine—is this: *we cannot know what will become of our children.* This is what I mean when I say it might even be dangerous to desire particular outcomes for our children, because the almost inevitable truth is that at least some of our desires will remain unfulfilled. Ever since Icarus disregarded his father's advice and flew fatally close to the sun, children have surprised and defied their parents, and I sometimes think my greatest challenge is to not grant surprise and defiance the power to disappoint me.

So, yes, I cannot know what will become of my sons. But I also know what I have seen, which is that the more freedom and autonomy I allow my children to follow their passions and to learn on their own terms, the more passionate and eager to learn they become. The more engaged they become. And, inasmuch as I grant myself the same freedom and autonomy, the more engaged I become. The more I learn.

Since Penny and I cannot know what the future holds for our

sons, we have chosen to focus intently on what the present offers them, on how the small moments of their days can teach and nurture them in ways that are both intentional and, often as not, unintentional and entirely unexpected. We have chosen to educate Fin and Rye in the context of a life-learning process known colloquially as "unschooling." This means that our sons do not attend public or private school, and they do not follow a structured curriculum, unless exploring the fields and forests around our home can be considered a "curriculum." They are not assigned homework, and they do not take tests. Their performance is not graded, nor is it compared to the performance of their peers. They are not compelled to sit at a desk, or to study any particular subject for any particular period of time.

There is a popular perception linking homeschooling to religious beliefs. In a 2007 National Center for Education Statistics survey, 83 percent of homeschooling parents said that providing "religious or moral instruction" influenced their decision to educate at home. Of course, "moral instruction" can occur in the absence of religious instruction, so it's impossible to know with certainty if a full 80-plus percent of the estimated two million US homeschoolers are motivated by religion. What is indisputable, however, is the public perception that homeschooling families are, by and large, stridently, if not fundamentally, religious.

We do not identify with any particular religion (which does not mean we are not spiritual). In fact, I am not aware of a single homeschooling or unschooling family in our community—and there are many—that chooses home education in order to provide religious instruction. Perhaps our community is merely anomalous, or perhaps our experience is indicative of a shift in the broader community of homeschooling and unschooling families. Probably, it's a little of each. Whatever the case, it is clear that most of the homeschoolers we have contact with choose home education for roughly the same reason we do: their vision for what a child's education should and can be does not align with what the institutionalized educational system offers. Often, they are further motivated by a desire to spare their children the indignities they suffered at the hands of the public school system.

The first known recorded use of the term *unschooling* came in 1977, in the second issue of a magazine called *Growing Without Schooling*: "GWS will say 'unschooling' when we mean taking children out of school, and 'deschooling' when we mean changing the laws to make schools non-compulsory and to take away from them their power to grade, rank, and label people i.e. to make lasting, official, public judgments about them."[1]

Growing Without Schooling was published by the late John Holt, an educator and author of the seminal *How Children Fail* (along with ten other books on the subject of children and education), which forwards Holt's observation that children are innately intelligent and inclined to learn. The problem, according to Holt, is that these innate qualities are actually stunted by institutionalized education, which is simply unable to serve the individual child in the context of its need to usher large groups of youth through a standardized, performance-based curriculum. Apparently, at least a few people agree, because *How Children Fail* has sold over one million copies.

Holt was a proponent of both homeschooling and unschooling, which are understandably often confused and thought to be one and the same. This is because unschooling generally occurs at home and can rightly be considered a subset of homeschooling. But unschooling is also very different from traditional homeschooling, which relies on textbooks, study time, and in some cases, prepackaged curriculums. I don't mean to suggest that Fin and Rye do not spend plenty of time with their noses in books, or that they don't study things. On both accounts, they very much do. But the subjects of their study are extensions of their natural interests and passions. These subjects are not assigned to them; they are *chosen* by them. It is within the context of these choices—of their personal interests and passions—that they learn the rote, essential skills such as math and spelling which enable them to function in the world.

Perhaps the best way to clarify the connection between unschooling and homeschooling is to understand that all unschooling is homeschooling, but not all homeschooling is unschooling. It should also be said that the two are not mutually exclusive; indeed, we know many families that combine elements of both unschooling and more traditional homeschooling. One of the beautiful things about choosing to educate your children at home is that it affords you the freedom to explore and experiment. And, not incidentally, it allows you to observe your children, because you cannot truly know how your child responds to a particular learning style unless you are there to witness its effects.

Of the educational options available to parents in America, unschooling is surely the least formal and structured. For precisely this reason, it is also the most difficult to describe with any accuracy, if for no other reason than that it has no exact definition. Wikipedia calls it "a range of educational philosophies surrounding the primary belief that education is a greater undertaking than school," which I suppose is close enough, although the word *range* certainly leaves plenty open to interpretation. But then, that's sort of the point: Unschooling cannot and should not adhere to any particular definition. It should be as fluid, imprecise, and individualized as the families and children practicing it. In this regard, it is the antithesis of contemporary institutionalized education, with its strict adherence to schedule, standardized testing, and age-group learning. The definition Penny and I have settled on is "learning through living." It is perhaps no more precise than what Wikipedia offers, but it feels most accurate and honest to us. Finlay and Rye live their lives. And as they live, they learn.

Having spent the past few paragraphs attempting to define *unschooling,* I must now admit I don't even *like* the term all that much. To me, it suggests undoing and rejection, when in fact we strive for a style of learning that is active and inclusive, that encourages engagement and leverages a child's natural curiosity and love of learning to nourish body, mind, and spirit. If that sounds far-fetched, I contend it is only because we have come to expect so little of our children's education.

Furthermore, we are not undoing school; Fin and Rye have never even been to school. There is nothing to undo. And while they do not attend a formal educational institution, we are not so much rejecting this option as actively choosing an alternate path. In fact, we are grateful for our town's public school and for what it brings to our community. Are there problems inherent in institutionalized education? Obviously, I believe there are. But I am not blind to the fact that home education is simply not an option for many parents, even if it might be their preference (this fact, which is directly related to issues of income and debt and other cultural expectations surrounding success, will be a subject of discussion in further chapters). Given this reality, I am extremely thankful that at least our community has the option of keeping its school-aged children in town.

So I describe and use the term *unschooling* with a slight sense of unease, simply because I do not believe it is an accurate description of what we are actually doing. Likewise, I'm pretty sure it's not an accurate description of what most unschooling families are doing, although I suppose I should leave that up to them to decide. But as many misgivings as I have about its use, there are three things the term *unschooling* does very well. First, it is concise. To describe our educational path with full accuracy would require a lot more than a single word (in fact, it appears that it requires an entire book!). Second, it is evocative. Almost everyone has associations—some pleasant, some not so much—with school. Simply because the term includes the word *school,* it is almost guaranteed to trigger an emotional response. And third, it demands attention, particularly in a culture that places so much emphasis on education. "Unschooling? What's that?" At which point, I am always happy to provide a greatly expanded definition of my sons' learning.

For all these reasons, and because I have yet to settle on a better term, I will continue to use the word *unschooling* to describe how my sons learn.

When I explain my children's unconventional educational path, I am often confronted with skepticism. "What if they want to be doctors?" people say. "How do they learn?" I am asked. "What if they want to go to college? Don't you worry about socialization?" I have heard these questions so often that it is almost as if I can see the thought as it migrates from brain to tongue. I can hear the question before the question has been asked.

The answers to these questions are at once simple (respectively: "If they want to be doctors, they will." "They learn because learning cannot be helped." "If they want to go to college, no one will be able to stop them." And "No, we are not worried about their socialization. Don't you worry about what schoolchildren are socialized *to*?") and complex. They are complex because so much of what we want for Fin and Rye and so much of what we want for ourselves cannot rightly be measured by the contemporary metrics of achievement. Every so often I think of the fact that Penny and I have chosen to exchange the security of moneyed wealth for the freedom to pass our days with as much autonomy as possible. Or the fact that our days are full of labor, of muscles made sore by long hours gathering firewood or stacking hay bales, sweat accumulating on our brows before the sun has even cleared the eastern horizon. Every so often, most often in the midst of some chore turned tedious by repetition and fatigue, I find myself thinking, "I don't have to do this." And then: "Is there something wrong with me that I want to?"

There is not, of course, and whatever fleeting moments of doubt I might experience are the result of allowing those voices and the well-meaning logic they convey—that we should worry that somehow our sons will not find their way into whatever career they desire, or that we'd be better served by taking steady jobs that could afford us the luxury of hiring out whatever unpleasant tasks need doing—to ring louder than the beliefs and experiences that guide us and bring so much beauty and balance to our days.

In both my family and in others, I have seen that parental expectations for childhood education are often corrosive to living with that sense of balance, as we allow ourselves to become swept into the river of extracurricular activities and expanded "opportunities." We do this with only the best of intentions, believing that such things will advantage our children, without considering the toll these activities and opportunities extract, the hours and days spent scurrying and hurrying, too pressed for time to simply sit and enjoy the spectacle of a setting sun or the warm wetness of a July rain shower.

All of this does not mean you must be a parent to appreciate these ideas, in part because this book is not solely about children, but also because children need the support and love of many more people than just their parents. The role of mentors in a child's community is rarely spoken of and, in fact, has all but disappeared. True, some communities offer mentoring programs, but they tend to be reserved for children whose home life defines them as being "in need." The reality is that all of our children are in need of meaningful, mutually respectful relationships with adults and elders to facilitate learning and help children understand their role in their communities and, by extension, the world.

As I will discuss in more detail later, we have gone to great lengths to seek out mentors for Fin and Rye, and the critical importance of their role in our sons' lives cannot be overstated. In fact, the critical importance of their role in Penny's and my lives cannot be overstated, in no small part because the mentors we have found are drawn to the relationship through a passionate embrace of the specific knowledge and experience they embody, but also a sense of their responsibility to pass this knowledge along. After Rye recently decided to take a break from banjo lessons, his music teacher, Sarah, reminded him that she would always be available to help. "Even if it's twenty years from now, you can call me with any questions, whether it has to do with music or not," she said. And with that offering, she demonstrated the generosity this passing on requires, the hours spent in the company of our sons, the slow transference of skill and wisdom and, as important as the taught skill itself, an ethos of sharing.

Having chosen such an unconventional path in both the manner we educate our sons and the way we pass our days, growing most of our food and remaining close to our home, there are times it feels to me as if my family's voice is lost in the crowd, and it can occasionally feel as if we occupy a lonely space. I do not mean "lonely" in the sense of lacking meaningful personal relationships, but in a broader cultural sense of living out-of-step with so many common goals and expectations. We drive decades-old cars with curmudgeonly contentment, and our thrift-store shirts bear patches on their patches, small scabs of cloth to cover the wounds inflicted by our labors. We tend to measure our wealth in terms of trees planted, time spent wandering the woods, and meals taken as a family. We do not earn very much money, and we do not care to, in large part because we believe that whatever time we might devote to earning money is generally worth more than anyone can pay us. There is a certain sociocultural isolation inherent in these choices, although I have noticed that the more fervently we embrace them, the more frequently we seem to connect with others who are making similar choices.

For their part, Fin and Rye seem generally unconcerned that they might be perceived as different. Recently, we attended an outdoor concert in a small city. The boys wore frayed camouflage pants, rubber barn boots, dangling belt knives, and—the pièce de résistance—a pair of felted wool caps they'd made of fleeces shorn from our sheep.

"Everyone is staring at us," said Fin after half an hour or so.

"Does it bother you?" I asked.

"No, I think it's hilarious." Then he ran off to be stared at some more.

This sense of being out of step is one of the challenges I face in my life and in the principles I apply to raising my children: to not lose sight of my truth in a world that in so many ways tells me it is false. There is little support for our choices in the mainstream economy and in the omnipresent messaging that supports this economy, and I believe there is little support for our choices precisely because there is little profit to be realized from them. The decision to revere our time more than money, or the things money can buy, is not profitable for anyone but us. The decision to remain largely at home, or in our immediate community, finding our inspiration and entertainment in the people and natural world surrounding us, is not profitable for anyone but us. The decision to invest in our relationships—not merely with other people but with the plants and animals surrounding us—is not profitable for anyone but us. The decision to simply be discerning—about what we buy, how we pass our time, what influences we allow to shape our lives—does not line anyone's pocket.

In this regard, this book performs one more function, albeit a decidedly self-serving one: It is a reminder to myself that just because the path we are following frequently deviates from the norm, we are not crazy. It is a reminder to act from the place of clarity that tells us that the world we imagine is not impossible, impractical, or illogical, as individuals or as a collective. In fact, it is precisely the opposite: it is reasonable. Beauty, kindness, generosity, abundance, and connection are products of profound reason. They are the only rational response to a world that so freely offers these qualities. They are all around us, embodied by both humans and nature, and I owe my children the opportunity to recognize this fundamental truth.

Over the years, I have observed something astounding. The more Penny and I provide our boys the opportunity to view the world in these terms, the more they reciprocate by offering the same opportunity to us. I remember a morning last summer, when Rye called to me through the open kitchen window, to where I stood, washing egg yolk off the breakfast dishes. "Come outside, Papa," he said. "Come look at this!" My boy was bent over the lifeless body of a star-nosed mole, a victim of our cats' predatory instincts. He showed me the moles' front paws, with their talon-like toes. He showed me the small appendages that ringed its snout, twenty-two in total. Later, we learned that the mole uses the 25,000 sensory receptors on these appendages to find and identify food. "That's amazing," said Rye, and we joked about what I'd look like with twenty-two tentacles protruding from my face. "Not much different," said my son, and I feigned offense.

Or I consider all the times Fin has returned from one of his woods rambles with a hatful of wild edibles. He brings fiddlehead ferns, blackberries, spruce gum, and honey mushrooms. He brings goatsbeard and toothwort. Since he rarely travels without a length of fishing line and a hook tucked into a pocket, maybe a pair of brookies, their skin wet and glistening. He builds a fire and cooks the fish on a hot rock until the flesh is white and flakey and falls away from the bone.

Without my sons, I would not have known of such a creature as the star-nosed mole, and those twenty-two tentacles. I might have known of fiddleheads and blackberries, but not of spruce gum. Certainly not of goatsbeard and toothwort. I would not have known how to cook a fresh-caught trout on a hot rock, or that the world even held such possibilities. Ever since that morning Rye showed me the mole, I occasionally think of those 25,000 sensory receptors and I wonder how many of my own receptors have gone dormant from lack of use. I marvel at how many of them my sons have helped me coax back to life. How many more are just waiting for the right combination of factors to awaken, to whisper stories about how the world is and how I might find my place within it?

And I realize that my failure to hear these whispered stories is the direct result of perceiving myself as standing apart from others and from the natural world. But of course I do not stand apart; none of us do. We are all interconnected and interdependent, and because of this, we are all only as rich as we enrich those around us. I did not learn this in school. I learned it from my children.

Overseers

In middle March I walk the upper pasture, stumbling under the weight of a pair of five-gallon buckets sloshing sap. The ground is nearly bare; the winter past was a feeble, fleeting thing, almost dreamlike in its rapid passing. Did it really happen? Was I really there? Why, I got the plow truck stuck only once, and two full rows of firewood remain in the shed. I'll be glad for them come fall.

A gallon of sap weighs eight pounds, and I carry ten gallons (or maybe nine; I've lost some over the bucket rims). Seventy, eighty pounds. Not so much, but the far taps are a quarter mile down the field, hung from the old maples that define the border between our land and our neighbor Melvin's dairy farm. They are big and graceful trees, overseers of decades and generations, and I cannot help thinking of all the cows that have loafed in their shade. I cannot stop myself thinking of all the storms they've survived, all the haying seasons they've known. The horse-drawn mowers, then the old Fords and Masseys, and now Melvin's big New Holland that can lay down the entire field in an afternoon. And every year, they give their sap. Am I honoring or exploiting them by accepting this gift? Strange how it can sometimes seem as if there's not much difference between the two.

Still, it humbles me to consider all they have seen and all they have given, as if these somehow juxtapose each other in a way that makes me unworthy of their gift. I am glad for the toil: the trudging through the late-February snowpack to drill and tap and hang, and now the daily shoulder-burning haul up the field to the small evaporator, fed with lengths of slabwood pulled off the sawmill as we boil down to the sweet essence of it all.

Halfway home. I stop at another tree, but of course the buckets are too full. I'll have to come back. Down in the valley, I hear the distant whine of a two-stroke engine, either an end-of-season snowmobile run along some shaded ribbon of snow or an early-season dirt bike. The noise fades into the distance and I can hear the high-pitched bleating of the lambs in the barn and I know they are running to and fro, energized by the warmth and sun and perhaps some instinctual knowledge that soon they will be turned out to the season's first tender shoots.

I set the buckets on the ground and for a minute, maybe two, I allow my mind to return to the previous morning. It was a cold one, barely a dozen degrees above zero and not yet full light when Rye slipped outside. The boy has caught the "fever," which is the preferred colloquialism for the affliction that strikes a certain subset of the population that will spend the latter half of March bloodletting the sugar maple trees. The fever is common as mud around here; we have neighbors whose livelihood is utterly dependent on the annual sap run, who for three or four weeks every year don't sleep more than a few hours per night, having spent the previous eleven months preparing for these hazy, exhausted days. We see them in town, at the post office or the hardware store, and the circles under their eyes tell us everything we need to know about what sort of season it's been. The bigger the circles, the better the sap's running, because of course no sugar maker worth his salt will rest when there's syrup to be made.

For the past month, Rye has been amassing his own pile of slabwood scraps, and yesterday he arranged a small stone fire pit, over which he'll boil away the thirty-nine parts of water necessary to glean one part of syrup. Concerned that Fin might beat him to the more productive trees before he got a chance to have at them, Rye marked his territory with strands of red yarn days ago.

It looked as if the trees wore necklaces around their trunks. "Those are my trees," he told Fin, as serious as if his livelihood depended on it, and Fin said OK, fine, whatever, he'd find his own.

One morning after chores, with Rye already stoking his fire and tendrils of steam just beginning to rise off the pot he'd appropriated for the task, I followed my son's tracks through the waning snowpack, just to see which trees he'd tapped. ("That way," was all he'd told me when I'd asked, pointing a gloved hand. Rye takes after Penny in that he rarely uses more words than necessary. Someday he might understand what a gift this is.) Down past the pond, over the hill at the pond's western shore, up the hill after that, and finally, down into the woods, the pitch so steep I had to slide down it on my ass. There, he'd drilled holes into nearly a dozen trees, a small copse of maples so tucked away I hadn't even known it existed. It was more than a quarter mile from his fire pit, and the haul—on some days, dozens of gallons—would be mostly uphill.

Down in the woods, I remembered a story Penny had told me a few days prior, how when she was driving Rye home from his weekly banjo lesson, she mentioned that there were times she still wished to travel. Penny's always been like that; when we met, she'd just returned from a year of backpacking and ranch work in Australia and New Zealand, and she can't quite pluck out the last few strands of wanderlust woven into her DNA. Someday, after the boys are grown, I'll probably wake up to a note on the kitchen counter: "Pack your bags. We're going to Africa." Anyway, Rye said sure, he'd be fine with some travel, no problem. "But we have to be home for sugarin' and haying," he implored. "I can't miss those."

Late that afternoon, I visited my son again. I kissed his head, his hair damp from steam, tasting of smoke and maple. He'd sat by the hungry fire all day, feeding it whenever it began to wane. Now his pile of wood was nearly gone and the buckets of sap were nearly empty, those thirty-nine parts of water having evaporated as if they were nothing at all.

"How much do you think I'll get?" he asked, and I peered into his finishing pot, where perhaps a pint of almost-syrup roiled.

"I don't know," I replied, unsure of exactly how to break the news that his hours of labor and attention had been reduced to so little. I looked at my boy. His face was smudged with soot. I couldn't lie. "Maybe a pint?"

"Really? You mean a whole pint?" He tipped his face to me, beaming as surely as if I'd told him his haul would be measured in gallons rather than cups.

"Yeah," I said, grinning back at him. "A pint. A whole pint."

2

Coming to the Land

IN ANY GIVEN AUTUMN in northern Vermont, there comes a day when the full intention of the approaching season becomes clear. On this day, a biting wind might blow, or a heavy rain might fall, or the air might carry the soft, uncommitted flakes of first snow meandering their way earthward. On this day, the sun may even shine, but there will be a certain slant to the light that speaks of transition. You may not recognize this day when it arrives; you may think it just another in a string of autumn days, its character and intent no more defined than those that came before and those that will follow. But in hindsight you will know differently. In hindsight, you will recognize it as the day the soft meat of summer was cleaved from the hard bone of winter.

It was on just such a day in the fall of 1996 that Penny and I first walked the land we would eventually purchase. It was a day of mottled browns and grays, the colors tempered by the season and a low ceiling of impassive clouds. A few stubborn leaves clung to the trees, unwilling to relinquish their thinning grip on life, but even they'd gone dull. Every day, a few more of them fell. Only the birches, slender and white as bones, seemed to harbor any color.

The property comprised a bit more than forty acres of field and forest on the outskirts of the northern Vermont town of Cabot. It sloped to the southwest, its downward pitch interrupted by frequent rises and small plateaus, as if the land were in no hurry to get where it was going. From its height we could see across a valley to the farm one ridge top over, where Holstein and Jersey cows dotted a landscape at the midpoint of its annual metamorphosis from summer's lush abundance to the full barrenness of winter, like a butterfly folding itself back into its cocoon.

Maybe you've heard of Cabot. If so, it's probably only because it is home to the eponymous creamery, the recipient of numerous cheese-making awards since its inception in 1918. "World's Best Cheddar!" is what the trucks say, and although I have not sampled all the cheddars of the world, I have no reason to disbelieve them. Cabot is also home to what is quite possibly the highest number of dairy farms per capita in the United States. In this town of 1,400 residents, give or take a few, there are an even dozen dairies. The smallest of these is populated by fewer than twenty milk cows; the largest, a bit more than seventy. Follow any road in this town long enough, and you'll pass a herd of cows. Follow it farther, and you'll pass another.

The land Penny and I walked that day sits directly between two of these dozen farms, one comprised of a bit more than a hundred acres and the other of nearly three hundred. Accessing the property meant passing through a crude gate of rusted barbed wire and weather-grayed cedar posts, before traveling across a hilltop hayfield and directly through a small herd of Holsteins that retreated from our outstretched hands. *High mowing* is the term farmers once used for these elevated hayfields, the ones with sweeping views, the ones that never flooded, the ones that, when standing at their apex, could make you feel as if the entire world unfurled from the very spot you'd planted your feet. Although we didn't know it then, the two herds—the one we passed through and the one we viewed from a distance—were owned by two brothers. Rusty and Melvin are their names, and they'd once farmed together but had long since split to run their individual ridgetop operations, the valley running like a river between them.

I carry another memory from that October day nearly two decades ago. Penny and I were pushing through a patch of raspberry whips, bent and fallow in the late-autumn chill. They were wet, and so were we because it had started raining, cold enough that it verged on snow. Above the whips, the sky was turning darker and denser, impenetrable as a bank vault. At the edge of the whips, to our right, a rusted barbed wire fence hung loosely from rotted posts. The wire followed the serpentine contours of the land, or it would have if it was still taut. But now the failing strand of metal dipped and rose randomly; in places it was broken, and long sections were simply missing.

I turned to Penny, and before I could even speak, I saw the smile wrapped around her face, saw how her eyes had taken on a sheen of excitement. "I love it," I said, a whisper so that the realtor, a dozen steps ahead of us, wouldn't overhear. We didn't want to show our hand just yet. We didn't want him to see us for the hopelessly smitten suckers we were. I whispered again: "I *love* it." Penny only nodded, but it was an emphatic nod, and her eyes widened even more, and I thought, "This is it." We made an offer that afternoon.

It is only in hindsight that I can grasp how profoundly I underestimated this land and how it would influence my life in ways I could never have foreseen. But how could I have known? I had not yet strung my own fence, or cared for the animals it would contain. I had had not yet built the house and laid the floor onto which I would see my sons be born, had not yet watched them climb into the apple trees we planted the day after we took title to the land. Those trees are more than fifteen years old now, and my sons shimmy high into the branches, picking unripe fruit along the way. "Don't you want one, Papa?" they tease, dropping a smooth, sour orb into my hands. I take a bite and make a show of spitting it out. They laugh and laugh.

Can a piece of land really shape a person in a manner that is unique to it? I believe this is true, but perhaps I do not give myself enough credit, because of course just as the land has crept up on us, we have crept up on it. We have built and planted and molded and dug. We have cut trees and stacked rocks and cleared fields and plowed furrows that from above look exactly like the open wounds they are. We have tried to treat this land with kindness and good intent, to act as partners more than overseers, but it occurs to me that we are not the best judges of our actions, and I trust that our mistakes will be forgiven.

And maybe the power this land wields over me is nothing more than whatever power I grant it. Or maybe it is not even power, a word that seems to have become associated with the hubris of military force and political influence. After all, it was Penny and I who chose the land; it was we who decided our lives would happen *here*, and not anywhere else. The land did not choose us. Or did it? Because who can say what truly compels us to make certain decisions. Is it always reason and logic? I know that often it is, and that often our choices come attached to a range of foreseeable outcomes, from which it is entirely possible to discern between the favorable and the unfavorable. But I wonder if sometimes our decisions are built upon something less tangible and connected to the realm of logic.

It was not as if we couldn't imagine the particular outcomes that might evolve from choosing this piece of land. Indeed, we could, and the yearning for these specific outcomes had, at least in part, led us to this property in the first place. These were the things we talked about in the evenings, in the damp confines of the $100-per-month cabin we'd rented as part of a campaign of extreme thrift launched years prior in hopes of saving as much of our meager income as possible toward our home-to-be. Lying in the smoky half-light of a flickering candle, we spoke of gardens and chickens and views and the privacy to splay our unclothed bodies across the grass on the first warm day of summer. "A pond!" Penny exclaimed. "We must have a pond!" and I agreed, because of course we must have pond. It was unthinkable that we wouldn't. We talked about the house we would build, how it would be small and simple. Cool in summer, warm in winter. Welcoming. Sturdy. Ours. Were we being idealistic? Well, maybe. Yes. But then, we'd been living in a decomposing cabin. Did we not deserve a little idealism? We did. We very much did.

We spoke of all these things, and our words carried certain assumptions about the property we would buy. That there would be open land to be plowed and tilled and sown. That there would be forest to provide firewood and sanctuary to wildlife and ourselves. That it would not be flat, but instead reveal its curves, along unfurling contours defined by geologic events long before our time and far beyond our capacity to imagine. We were not yet speaking of a family, but it is fair to say that children were also assumed. But at the time, the idea of children was too massive a force to be reckoned with, not unlike the geologic events that had shaped land we did not yet own.

So did we choose this land, or did this land choose us?

To this day, I am not sure.

FITTING INTO TREES

On an early February morning, I rise early, propelled by the feeling that too many days have passed since I've greeted the rising sun with sweat on my brow, so I coax the fires to life, slip out the door, and step into my skis. It is still dark and an even zero degrees, but it's been the sort of winter that makes a zero-degree morning feel like just the way things are, so I am not cold. I glide up past the barn and the still-prone cows, and I imagine them turning their shaggy heads toward me in greeting or maybe just curiosity, but it is too dark to know if they so much as glance my way.

Out on Melvin's field, at the height of the land, I slot into the packed depression left by the big, lugged tire of his New Holland on his way to gather firewood the afternoon before. The sky is bluing ever so slightly above me, and I ski as fast as the cold snow will let me. Over by the old hollow oak I can see down to Melvin's barn. Light shines through a window. Chore time. It is almost six A.M., so I know Melvin is probably feeding out at that very moment. Understanding this reminds me of Thanksgiving, when we'd all been sitting around our big farmhouse table, shifting ever so slightly in our chairs to relieve the post-meal discomfort of expanded bellies pressing against waistbands. We'd had one serious cold snap already, and I said something like "I hope it's a good, hard winter." Melvin didn't miss a beat: "Spoken like someone who makes his living at a desk," he said, and he was grinning like he does when he's heckling me but also knows he's speaking the truth and furthermore knows that I know he's speaking the truth. It's a tidy arrangement, really.

That old oak. The boys used to squeeze themselves into it all the time. They'd spend hours in and around that tree, lost to their imagining. We'd read Jean Craighead George's classic story *My Side of the Mountain*, about a young man who spends a winter living inside a hollow tree, and I suppose that had something to with the boys' fascination, but I bet they would have found that tree no matter what.

Just a few days prior, Fin told me that he and Rye can't fit into the oak anymore. Isn't that the way it goes. I suppose it would've made me sort of sad if it didn't reveal the simple fact that they still wanted to fit into it. That they'd tried. And it occurred to me that trying to fit inside a hollow tree might be as important as actually fitting into it.

The tree's days are numbered. It's going in Melvin's furnace, if not this winter, then next. If not next winter, the one after that. That's OK. My boys don't fit in there anymore, and a furnace doesn't run on sentiment.

By the time I return home, I've gotten the sweat I'd wanted. I can taste it on my upper lip. I ski past the cows again, and this time, I can see that they do look my way. Wanting hay. Wanting fresh water. I go into the house, remove my ski boots, change into my chore boots, and step back outside.

3

The View

IF I STAND AT THE HEIGHT of our land looking west, this is
what I see: At my feet, the steep slope of pasture falling away from
me, an expanse of grass that unrolls, carpet-like, for a few hundred
yards before running into the line of trees that demarcate the forest's edge. To my left, the pasture extends southward for a quarter
mile or so; to my right, it is hemmed by our house and barn, as well
as two small outbuildings that serve as a rudimentary workshop
and a three-sided shed to shield the cows from the weather. A long
greenhouse protrudes at a right angle from the southern wall of our
home. From certain vantage points, it reminds me of a nose.

A couple of hundred feet below the greenhouse, I see a small, ter-
raced orchard, and below that, a copse of sugar maple trees. There are
perhaps twenty-five in total and, with the benefit of the giant maples that line the southeastern boundary of our property (as I stand
atop that knob of pasture, these are behind me, running along a row
that follows our pasture line to the south), they provide the half-
dozen or so gallons of maple syrup my family consumes each year.
Below the copse of maples, there is a pond, which a neighbor dug for
us four years ago. It is fed by three separate springs, and even in August it is so cold that jumping from one of the rocks at its shore feels
like a small feat of bravery. On those midsummer days that dawn hot
and hazy and finish even hotter and hazier, I am often in the pond
no fewer than four times: once before breakfast, once prior to lunch,

once after evening chores, and once more as the light is leaving the sky, a cooling dunk to ease the transition from wakefulness to sleep. I shuck my sweat-damp clothes in the expanse of grass that leads to the pond's edge, step onto my favorite jumping rock, gather my insignificant reservoir of courage, and leap. Because I do not really like to swim per se, I am generally back on shore within minutes, drying myself with my T-shirt so that it might absorb some of the frigid pond water.

There are two small rafts wedged against the shore. Fin and Rye built them, hauling small-diameter fir logs to the ponds' edge, where they used handsaws to cut them into equal lengths, and fashioned decks of slabwood. They ride the rafts for hours, poling themselves across the pond, lost to the world beyond the water's lapping fringe. Watching them, I remember the week in January during which I read *Huckleberry Finn* aloud, the three of us curled into the tattered sofa near the woodstove, chortling at Huck and Jim's antics. And I remember the raft my father and I built when I was their age, and how I floated on the pond behind the rental house we lived in at the time, everything forgotten but the small square of slippery wood beneath my feet and the murky water it floated on.

What else can I see? I can see the ninety-something blueberry bushes we planted sixteen years ago, before we'd even broken ground on our shelter. This struck me as nothing short of insane— after all, we were at the time living in the aforementioned rental shack—but as is so often the case, Penny knew better than I. "In five years, you'll be really glad we did this," she said, and I can't remember my exact reply—probably something snarky like "Yeah, in five years I'll be really glad to have a roof that doesn't leak"—but of course she was right. Penny is graced with the ability to envision a future I can only blindly lurch toward; she knew that bareroot blueberry whips take at least five years to produce and she knew of the Chinese proverb that says, "The best time to plant a tree is twenty years ago. The second best time is now."

When I think of those berries, I recall how it used to be that every summer around the first of August, one of the boys would come running from the patch with a handful of half-ripe specimens in his hand. "Papa, they're ready, they're ready! These are for you!" he'd yell, and I'd chuckle to myself, because I knew his belly was full of the ones that really *were* ripe. In truth, the boys' enthusiasm has hardly diminished; at eight and eleven, they still come running from the patch, still calling out that the berries are ready. They no longer hoard the ripest ones; at some point over the past few years, their sense of justice and generosity has evolved so that their grubby-palmed offerings are deeply blue and plump, a full expression of what a fresh blueberry can be, made all the sweeter by the eleven months that have passed since the last of the previous season's berries were coaxed from the vine.

Just before the blueberry patch, atop one of the few relatively flat expanses on our property, there is a large garden. Actually, it is one of three gardens we tend, which in total comprise maybe a quarter acre of cultivated land. The garden near the blueberries is called the "wedding field," so named because it is where we pitched the tent that provided shade and shelter for the friends and family who attended our wedding in 1998, the summer after we closed on the land. There is also a garden just above the pole barn where we store hay (the "upper garden"), and one immediately to the north of the house (the "lower garden"). Increasingly, the spaces between the gardens are being populated by fruit and nut trees, along with other food-bearing plants, as we transition toward a landscape that is rooted in permaculture design and theory, which models natural ecosystems to create largely self-maintaining food production.

By the time they were four, the boys had their own rows in the garden. They painted wooden signs and mounted them on stakes at the end of their rows: "Garden of Fin" read the first, installed when Rye was still an infant, not yet old enough to contribute. The second reads, "Rye and Fin Garden," the lettering completed before the boys understood the grammatical rules of possession. In the early years, we helped them plant and tend their rows, but this is no longer necessary. Now they harvest baskets of garlic and potatoes from seed stock they planted themselves. They contribute a portion of their bounty to the family food stores; the rest they sell or trade away with friends and mentors, receiving in exchange the small tools of their passions: a flint and steel, a handful of arrows, a small-bladed hook knife for carving the hollow of a bowl or spoon.

We did not overtly teach them how to grow things; we merely incorporated them into every aspect of the process since before they could walk. Their first sandbox was perched at the corner of the upper garden. There they dug and burrowed while Penny and I weeded. By the time Fin was two, he was helping plant potatoes. "Night, night, 'tatoes," he'd say as he pushed the soft soil over the sprouted quarters that would become the smooth, hard orbs we'd uncover six months later and store for the coming winter. We granted the boys unfettered access to the gardens, and I'd like to say we did so without hesitation. But the truth is, this was hard for us, and particularly so for Penny. The gardens have long been a point of pride for her, and to see Fin rearranging the stakes that identified her trial varieties, or to watch the boys trod heedlessly through a bed of just-emerged beets was an exercise in patience that sometimes felt too strenuous to maintain. But our desire for the boys to feel at home in the gardens was even stronger, so we bit our tongues, and replanted in their wake.

Depending on the season, from where I stand atop that knoll I might see seven or eight cows grazing on the pasture, and I might see a pair of pigs splayed across the ground, warming their expansive bellies in the sun. I might see the fifty or so broiler chickens we raise each year for our freezer, pecking and squawking and strutting in that frantic, head-forward way chickens strut, as if each step were a recovery from a near fall. There's a good chance our dog, Daisy, will be lurking about; she's a Bluetick Coonhound and prone to manic bursts of activity, punctuated by the sort of long, untroubled hours of slumber that could drive an insomniac mad with envy. Because I can almost reach out and touch it, I can definitely see the wind turbine that sits atop a sixty-five-foot tower and makes a pleasing whirring noise as its blades revolve; our array of solar photovoltaic panels is slightly farther out of reach, but it is visible, too.

Everywhere I look, I see evidence of friends and family. I remember raising the windmill with our friend Jim, and I remember how one of the guylines failed, how we heard the horrible hiss of the rope unfurling and we yelled and dove as the tower crashed to the ground.

And I remember how Penny's brother and his wife helped lay the plastic over the greenhouse. It was windy that day and the wind got under the plastic, threatening to send it sailing into the trees and perhaps us with it, but we managed to wrestle it down just as dark came in full. There's the apple tree my mother planted back when Penny and I were still working on the shell of the house. There's the retaining wall made of huge slabs of fieldstone Melvin helped us gather and place with his big tractor. It took a full afternoon, and he wouldn't take any money. I think of our friend Bob and how he came every weekend for nearly a year. Could we have built this house without Bob's help? Maybe. Probably. But it surely wouldn't have been as much fun.

Our home is a traditional farmhouse style, with a steeply peaked roof, and already in spots the roofing tin is rusting. I suppose it will not be very many years before I will be compelled to replace the sheets of metal I so vividly remember installing. Below the roof, there are rough wooden clapboards and divided-light windows painted dark blue. Because the clapboards are unpainted and have therefore weathered over the years to a dull gray, our house probably looks older than it is. More than fifteen years after we broke ground, there remain certain unfinished aspects to the house—a missing piece of baseboard here, an unpainted surface there—that may or may not reach completion in our lifetime. The way I've come to look at it, these quirks add character to our home (and I'm fortunate that on most accounts, Penny agrees). They are evidence not merely of our home's imperfection but of ours as well, and in this regard, I view these flaws as an expression of our personalities.

What can't I see? I can't see very far into our woodlot, from which we harvest the five or six cords of firewood that heat our house every winter. Ash, maple, beech, yellow birch. I seek out the dead and dying, the weakest specimens among our woodlot's citizenry, and cleave them from the latticework of roots that runs beneath the soil. I drag the logs home behind the tractor and pile them for bucking and splitting on one of the Sunday mornings we reserve for processing firewood. Some families attend church; we split firewood, and again I see the imprint of the land on my sons in their progression as contributors to our family's heat source, from throwers of the smallest sticks to wielding the maul against the easy-splitting rounds of ash and birch. They have learned to pilot our old Ford pickup up the farm road, its rear springs sagging under the load, whichever boy is driving sitting straight and his chin tilted up so that he might see above the curve of the steering wheel.

I also can't see behind me, where Melvin's hayfield disappears over the eastern horizon. It's a wonderful thing, that field. In the spring, it is redolent with the manure he spreads, an odor that would be considered offensive only by those who do not understand the vibrancy it brings to a crop of hay. In the summer, Melvin's field is thick and green and lush and then, when he hays, nubby and shorn and less green. In the fall, after he has taken the second cutting of hay, he turns his milk cows out to graze on it, and the field is dotted with their great, lumbering forms, either standing with heads bent to the grass or lounging in the shade of a fence-line maple. At least a few mornings every fall, I'll see him just across our shared boundary, driving the cows down to his barn for morning milking as I tend to one chore or another, the foggy half-light of almost-dawn rendering him more as vague movement than any specific shape. But that stride: I'd know it anywhere. "Morning, Melvin," I'll say, no louder than necessary, the hour deserving the small respect of my restraint. "Morning," he answers back, as the fog swallows him.

In the winter, Melvin's field is covered with snow and we ski across it almost daily, faces tucked behind our collars to protect our cheeks from the prevailing wind. There is a soft rise that runs across the center of the field, and depending on where one stands, anything atop that rise is etched against the sky and there is nothing to suggest that stepping off the other side would be any different from stepping off the edge of the earth.

I also can't see our driveway, which parallels Melvin's field from the main road for a quarter mile. It is narrow, lined mostly by pine and balsam fir, and it is riddled with potholes, like earthen Swiss cheese. Every year, I fill in a few of the holes with crushed stone, and every year, more holes appear, like a geologic game of Whac-A-Mole. On both ends of our drive, there are short, steep hills that contribute to my miring the plow truck on a regular basis. This is an event I not so secretly covet, as it involves our tractor and a chain and a particular sort of crude, rural ingenuity ("From which angle shall I pull?" "Do I go forward or backward?" "Full gas or idle?" and so on) in which I like to think I specialize. The boys love to plow with me, and when I become stuck, they love to race back down the driveway, shouting my predicament into the thin winter air: "Papa's stuck! Mama, Papa's stuck!" This duty fulfilled, they spin around and run back to witness my antics and offer unsolicited advice.

I can't see the old sugarhouse foundation, a hundred years old or more, nestled into a stand of balsam down past the power line that traverses our property. I like that foundation. Like the failing perimeter fences that define our boundaries, it is a comforting reminder to me that nothing I am doing on this land is new. Nothing I am doing is out of the ordinary.

I often wonder about this land's imprint on my sons, and I consider how their immersion in nature—which this place enables to an extent that many would not—has become one of the nurtured parts of them, an environmental factor that will determine so much of how and what their lives will be. What parts of them are *them*—their innate nature, the cells and synapses, thoughts and emotions that cannot be influenced by place—and what parts of them are that same integration of land, spirit, thought, and emotion and even body that I know to be so strong a factor in my own life? How different might they be, in ways both subtle and profound, if they lived elsewhere? Would Rye still be so self-possessed? Still so drawn to labor, at seven years old already wearing holes in the palms of his leather work gloves? Would Fin still be so keen on the hunt, so primal in his curiosities? (He tells me what he's learned about how best to prepare field mice for eating. "You singe the fur right off them," he tells me. "They get sort of crispy.")

You might call our place a farm, or you might call it a homestead, or you might call it some combination of the two; there are no precise definitions for these terms, and that is fine by me. People often ask me to describe our property, and I just as often struggle with my reply, because it seems to me as if it defies easy categorization. We do not garner much income from our land. At most, a few thousand dollars per year. But then, we do not have to buy much food, either, and in this regard, we do realize a certain type of profit from our land and our efforts. And of course it has come to inform almost every aspect of our lives, from how Penny and I spend our days to how and even what Fin and Rye learn, hour by hour, day by day.

I would be remiss if I didn't briefly mention the land that surrounds our property, because it too has become a defining factor in our lives. It is our good fortune to live in a community that does not place much stock in No Trespassing signs, and we roam freely (permission having been granted, of course) across our neighbors' properties, seeking morel and chanterelle mushrooms, casting lines in prolific brook-trout streams, and exploring on our skis come winter. I know how rare this freedom has become, and how fortunate my sons are to have access to more than five hundred acres of field and forest, all of which unfolds literally from our doorstep. Over the years, their boundaries have steadily expanded, responsibility granted as it has been earned, and now it is common for them to wander miles at a time.

So. This is our place, to the extent that a place can ever be "ours"; I'm sometimes more inclined to think of our sense of ownership as being nothing more than an affectation. After all, we can only claim this land because somewhere far down the chain of ownership someone drove the native populations from it. Certainly we'll soon enough pass on from here, and until someone convinces me that an afterlife is an ironclad guarantee, I'm assuming we'll have no idea what or who will come to "own" this land next. Fin and Rye, presumably, but what they do with it will be entirely up to them and far beyond our capacity to influence, anyway.

In the meantime, our land and infrastructure are constantly evolving, either as a result of our intervention (over just the past four years, we've dug a pond, planted three small orchards, partially converted two acres of forest to pasture, and erected a pair of outbuildings), or the inevitable continuum of nature's process. This land, like all land, is in a constant state of change. There are the changes we have wrought, and there are the cyclical, generally predictable shifts inherent in each season, although these seasonal changes seem to be getting less and less predictable with each passing year.

And of course there are changes tied to events, like the storm one summer that brought down the old elm tree along the fence line we share with Melvin. "I'm sorry to see that elm go," I told Melvin the afternoon after the storm. We were standing in his barnyard, in our usual spot just outside the door of the milk room, both of us facing the town road at the other end of the yard. Melvin is shorter than me by nearly a foot, and wears a frayed baseball cap perpetually. Indeed, I'd known him for years before discovering he was mostly bald. "Me, too," he said, looking at me. "Me, too." Elm is not great firewood—full of moisture, prone to rot, hard to split—but I bucked the fallen tree into stove lengths anyway, half for Melvin and half for us. It burned begrudgingly, spitting water and sputtering. But it burned.

Less obviously, there is the unhurried, almost imperceptible change that must be measured in years, if not decades. An abandoned sugarhouse decays, leaving only a rusting arch, slowly returning to the soil, and around it, a rough rectangle of foundation stone, punctuated by towering trees. A hummock erodes, losing height at the rate of millimeters per annum, the same way a person begins to fold in on himself as age and gravity conspire. Sometimes I find myself wishing I could see our land long after I've died, to know what changes will come in my wake. But I know it's a silly wish and I do not hold on to it.

I am forty-two now, which is old enough to begin to understand how little I truly know. Sometimes, it seems as if I know less every day. But there is at least one thing I'm certain of, one thing that cannot be refuted, if only because I am presented with its evidence everywhere I turn. This place and I have shaped each other, one incorporated into the substance of the other, and both the opportunity to incorporate and the opportunity to be incorporated have defined me in ways I may never fully understand. Both are emblematic of a particular type of freedom, one that is becoming increasingly rare, as the very notion of place is usurped by transience. Transience holds its own sort of freedom, to be sure, a freedom of movement and change, but one that is so often mandated by forces that feel achingly beyond our control, as is so often the case when paying work is sought or other life circumstances intervene.

Have our decisions to live where and how we do and to educate the boys the way we do merely accentuated their inborn natures or have they come perilously close to defining them? An absolute answer cannot be known, and of course the question could apply to any child, reared in any environment. But there can be no denying that just as this place has shaped me, it is shaping my sons. The fact that Fin and Rye feel the pull of this land is as undeniable as the very fact of their existence.

Someday, of course, that pull may wane, or the pull of another place may prove stronger. That is OK. That is the natural order of things. But what the shaping this land has done will not be easily eroded. Whatever else my boys forget, they will remember where they came from. There is no doubting that.

CHOOSING FOR OURSELVES

My children have enormous freedom to do as they please. This is by design; we have engineered it into our lives, the way most people make room for a career, or strategize their retirement. Most mornings after chores and breakfast, the boys set out on some adventure or another, into the woods or down the field. Usually they do this together, although it is not infrequent that one returns before the other, complaining of a grave injustice: Rye didn't want to pretend they were carrying a .30-30, and everyone knows you can't hunt deer with a .22. Rye put wet wood on the fire and it went out. Fin made Rye carry the heavy backpack. Like I said, grave, grave injustices. But they often disappear for hours, returning only when they become hungry or when whatever force that motivated their journey has waned.

"Where'd you guys go?" I'll ask, and the reply is often long and by necessity detailed: Down the snowmobile trail to Celley's stream, but the fish weren't biting, so up the banks of the stream onto the Ackermanns' land, then doubling back through the hayfield and Keith's sugarwoods, before returning to camp. "We saw moose tracks," Fin tells me. "Yeah," says Rye, "and the scat was fresh. Last night, probably. We found these, too." He reaches a grubby hand into a pocket, and for a moment, I'm almost afraid of what he'll extract—Moose poop? Something dead?—but it's only a handful of wild onions, small white bulbs we'll slice so thin they become translucent before frying them in butter.

From a parenting perspective, there is a downside to the tre-mendous degree of freedom they have been afforded: The boys have become rather discerning regarding how they spend their time. In short, when the occasion calls for them to do something they'd rather not do, they are not always accommodating. Part of this, of course, is simply a child's inability to grapple with time: What is happening right now is everything to a child. There is little aware-ness that it will pass, that something else will take its place. There is little capacity to understand that an unpleasant task is temporary, that its unpleasantness is a fleeting thing and, furthermore, only as unpleasant as it is believed to be.

Penny and I talk about this a lot. "Are we giving them too much freedom?" I ask, standing in the kitchen in the aftermath of a con-flagration with one of my sons or the other, often over a requested task deemed unworthy of their efforts. "I don't know," she says, and it's not a non-answer, because she doesn't know. Nor do I.

Depending on our mood, and the degree to which the boys have managed to invoke our ire, our perspective on their entitlement spans a broad chasm of possible outcomes. The worst of these, we figure, is that we've failed them completely and they will never amount to much of anything, being unwilling to do anything but what suits them in the moment. The best is that we are teaching them to be particular about how they pass their time, that time is a finite resource, and that this will serve them well as they go out into a world that does not encourage such discernment.

I suspect the truth is probably somewhere in the middle, if only because experience has taught me that this is where truth most of-ten lurks. They will, of course, need to learn how to accept that life will not always meet their expectations. They will benefit greatly if they learn that some of what will be required of them will not be pleasant. They will need to learn that what is not pleasant will be only as unpleasant as they allow it to be.

Still, I can't help but think of how my own sense of discernment over my time has shaped my life, and generally for the better. I did not like school, so I walked away from it. I did not like working for others, so I chose not to. I do not like to spend a lot of time indoors, so I don't. The truth is, I want to live the way I want to live, conventions be damned, and I can only hope for my sons to know they can be so free.

4

Drive

Just before I turned sixteen, in November 1987, my mother sold me her car. It was a ten-year-old Volkswagen Rabbit, the exact same yellow-tan hue as a newborn's soiled diaper. It had four forward gears, hand-crank windows, and an AM/FM radio, which emitted a buzzy squawk through its in-dash speakers. I paid my mother two hundred dollars for the car, a price my parents settled on because it fooled them into believing I'd actually earned the thing rather than had it dropped into my ungrateful adolescent lap.

Back in the day, those little Rabbits were prized by miscreant teens. They weighed hardly anything, particularly once a few Vermont winters' worth of rust had eaten away at their flimsy tin shells, and some of them—mine included—were equipped with 1.6-liter fuel-injected engines that could be revved to a racecar-like 7,000 rotations per minute. Most crucially, the Rabbits' emergency-brake handle activated the rear wheels rather than the front, a feature that enables the high-velocity, 180-degree turnaround skids that are a mainstay stunt of any newly licensed scoundrel.

I drove my new car heedlessly, with a juvenile's inflated confidence and arrogant disregard for law or safety, which probably does not surprise you. Mostly, I traveled the latticework of dirt roads around my childhood home, my friends and I shrieking along to the angst-ridden music of the era, which played through the buzzy speakers of an old boom box I'd appropriated for the task: Metallica,

Suicidal Tendencies, Bad Brains, Slayer. At the time, my favorite song was a Bad Brains number called "The Regulator." I played it over and over again, nodding my head to the heavy beat as the band's lead singer, H.R. (for Human Rights, naturally), railed against the despotic forces regulating and oppressing his existence.

One month after I took possession of my mother's car, with the ink barely dry on my driver's license, I dropped out of high school.

Did I hate school? Well, yes, I suppose so, but only in aggregate. There were elements of it I liked very much. For instance, I liked hanging out in the parking lot with my friends. That was a lot of fun, or at least, it fit my version of fun at the time. I liked Creative Writing, one of the few classes I rarely cut. I liked my physics class, not because I liked Physics (I flunked it, along with Algebra, Calculus, History, and French) but because Tom, my teacher, was something of an oddball. He smelled horrific, wearing the accumulation of his fetid perspiration like a badge of honor. But despite the odor, and despite my flailing half attempts to succeed in his class, there *were* compensations, such as the time he encouraged my friend Django and me to paint an old steel barrel with the international warning symbol for nuclear waste and leave it in a conspicuous place on school grounds. In no way could I discern how this had anything to do with physics.

"Why?" we asked him.

He raised his walrus-ian eyebrows into inverted V's. "To see what happens," he replied.

We jettisoned the barrel in a shallow depression at the edge of one of the playing fields, after which followed a sleepless night listening to the Bad Brains and fretting over the legal ramifications of creating counterfeit toxic waste. What special sort of wrath might the law reserve for a couple of sixteen-year-olds with an old barrel, a can of spray paint, and an ingrained sense of mischief? At two thirty A.M., in the lonely darkness of my childhood bedroom, my imagination ran toward long years of solitary confinement in the sort of juvenile facilities that are, at some point in the distant future, revealed to have been riddled with abuse.

The following morning, the barrel was gone. Django and I waited anxiously for news of its discovery, but none came, and for reasons I still do not understand, this delighted Tom.

Despite these shenanigans and despite the pleasure I derived from my creative writing class, the prevailing theme of my truncated high school career was one of simple boredom. And with it, a sense of my time being wasted, of my life slipping through my young fingers. In class after class, I slumped in my chair, quietly seething at my captors and, more broadly, at the unquestioned assumption that I should be held captive in the first place. Where was the relevance in what I was learning? In what ways might it inform and improve my life outside the context of school? It felt to me as if the entire experience was unfolding in a vacuum and that, once I graduated, the seal on the vacuum would burst, and I would be helplessly sucked into the real world, for which my schooling had done little to prepare me. I think this feeling frightened me, although I doubt I would have admitted so at the time.

Restlessly, I would shift my gaze from the algebraic equations scrawled across the chalkboard to the fields and forest and sky that for the majority of my waking hours remained achingly out of reach beyond the classroom's plate glass windows which, for all their transparency, felt like nothing so much as the bars of a prison cell. What was I looking for? Nothing in particular, frankly. Nothing more than simple escape, a refuge from captivity, where the information I was being forced to memorize and recite (as if the latter were proof of having learned something) felt as if it mattered only against the backdrop of school.

Out there was the world I wanted to know and understand. Out there was the tangible world, the world where knowledge and experience did not depend on memorizing what I was told to memorize, what the regulations told me I must learn, but on *doing*. I wanted to be out there, immersed in a world that made sense to me, that had not been reduced to formulas, equations, and rules. I wanted to explore and try and understand my connection to this world, and my place within it.

I recognize some of this only in hindsight, of course. The truth is, I was no more insightful than any other angst-ridden teenager trying to find his place in a world that seemed unaccommodating, if not inhospitable. It was not that I knew precisely what I wanted, because I did not. But I knew that what I'd been offered and compelled by both law and tradition to accept felt unnatural to me. It cut against the fibers of my being in a way that left me abraded and raw.

In his book *Free to Learn,* Peter Gray, a research professor in the Department of Psychology at Boston College, describes school this way:

> Everyone who has ever been to school knows that school is prison, but almost nobody beyond school age says it. It's not polite. We all tiptoe around the truth because admitting it would make us seem cruel and would point a finger at well-intentioned people doing what they believe to be essential . . . . A prison, according to the common, general definition, is any place of involuntary confinement and restriction of liberty. In school, as in adult prisons, the inmates are told exactly what they must do and are punished for failure to comply. Actually, students in school must spend more time doing exactly what they are told to do than is true of adults in penal institutions. Another difference, of course, is that we put adults in prison because they have committed a crime, while we put children in school because of their age.[1]

I do not think every child feels this way; indeed, some children seem to genuinely enjoy school. These are generally the same children that excel within the context of what it offers, and it's hard for me to discern which comes first, the excellence or the enjoyment. In other words, do they excel because they actually like what school has to offer them? Or do they like what school has to offer them because they excel, and are thus the recipients of all the associated benefits of their ability to comply and perform? Or maybe it is both.

Truth be told, I never was one of those children, nor did I have many, if any, friends who excelled in school. But it was not difficult to see how that cycle worked: The children who performed well in school received recognition and honors from teachers, parents, and the community at large. This recognition and these honors felt good, and so these children sought more of the same—who wouldn't? And as they continued to excel, they got better at excelling. They learned how the system works, and they trained themselves to perform in the context of that system. Furthermore, they took comfort in the knowledge that excellence in school foments a degree of security, both economically (admission to a good college and beyond that, whatever career path they might choose) and socially (more recognition and advancement based on that recognition).

My success or failure in school was dependent on my ability to follow a curriculum that felt as if it had very little to do with me as a human being. Certainly, it had not been designed by me or by anyone who had so much as met me. It was designed to a common denominator, and that common denominator was the assumption that someday, in the not-too-distant future, I'd graduate high school, continue on to college, and then, ultimately, settle into the career that would define what I would do and be for the rest of my life. Or until I got sick of being defined in this manner and found another job. It all felt irrelevant to my experience as a *person*.

I cannot remember precisely when I began to feel this way. Perhaps it was earlier than high school, but in any case, I would not have been able to articulate this sense of irrelevance. In grade school, where I was overweight and therefore unpopular, the proverbial (and in most cases, literal) last kid picked for any student-selected group activity, I still strove to meet the terms and conditions of my school-based identity. My desire to fit in was enormous, a hunger that could never be satisfied. I did not expect to be popular—few fat kids do—but I thought that if I worked hard enough at being relevant in the context of grade school's social mores, I might at least be accepted. So I wore the clothing I was supposed to wear, listened to the music I was supposed to like, and clumsily tried to play the games and sports I was supposed to play.

It never really worked, of course, perhaps in part because I bore the social burden of my weight and whatever awkwardness it had instilled in me, but also because my true interests lay elsewhere. I loved reading above all else, and most mornings I'd set my alarm clock to wake me at four thirty, which gave me two full hours to read before I had to gather myself for school. And despite my girth, I loved riding my bicycle. I made jumps in the driveway and rode over them for hours on end. I fantasized that someday my parents would move us to California, where I could ride year-round and where I'd blossom into a professional cyclist.

I cannot recall this period without circling back to my sons, whose freedom to immerse themselves in their true passions and identities occasionally delivers to me pangs of envy, as if there is still a piece of the outcast boy I was three decades ago trapped inside my chest. Or maybe there really *is* a piece of this boy inside me. Whatever the case, I find tremendous comfort in the knowledge that Fin and Rye are not burdened by the expectations of their peer group. No one tells them their pants are funny, so they unself-consciously wear the clothing Penny brings home from thrift stores: faded jeans, frayed jackets, socks with floral prints. No one tells them they're too fat or too skinny, too short or too tall, too slow or too weak, so they do not regard their physical characteristics and capabilities as being either flawed or lacking flaws, and I rarely hear them speak of others in these terms. No one tells them they should have a particular cell phone, or that they should watch a particular television show or movie, so they are free of the burden of desire for things they do not need or want. It is true that as they've grown older, they have become more aware of the material goods and cultural icons that captivate many of their peers, but they just don't seem to care. They are genuinely flummoxed that some of their friends choose to pass waking hours playing video games. "What's that about, anyway?" Fin asked me once. He'd just returned from a friend's overnight birthday party, where at the age of ten he'd played his first video games. "Seemed pretty boring to me," was his conclusion.

By high school, I had mostly shed the desire to identify with my classmates, and I had begun to understand that a meaningful life could be crafted outside the social mores and status of school. Does every high school student experience the internal turmoil and frustration I experienced? Of course not. Does every high-achieving student perform only for recognition and advancement? Of course not. I have no doubt that some students enjoy and perhaps even love learning in a structured, standardized fashion, and are fulfilled by what school can offer them. But my personal experience and observations—however anecdotal they might be—suggest that many, many more do *not* love learning in this manner and feel as if institutionalized learning does not honor them as people. If there is value in the standardized, performance-based curriculums utilized by the vast majority of schools, that value is realized primarily by the institutions themselves and by the economic and social structures that are fed by standardized learning.

The popular notion that these curriculums serve a so-called "greater good" is itself rooted in the flawed ideology of that greater good. What if that "greater good" isn't so good, after all? It also assumes, perhaps not overtly, but certainly inadvertently, that children have no other meaningful way to contribute to the portion of their community that exists beyond the classroom walls beyond fulfilling the expectations of these standardized curriculums. The irony is that the more we distance children from their broader communities by forcing them to attend school for the majority of their waking hours, the fewer opportunities they have to contribute to society in ways that cannot be measured by classroom performance. Consequently, the fewer opportunities society has to witness the ways in which children can contribute beyond the classroom. It is a self-perpetuating cycle.

To their immense credit, my parents were accepting of my decision to leave high school. I think they recognized that I was spinning my wheels. Were they disappointed and concerned? I know they were, and my mother still remembers the very moment she was able to relinquish control over my destiny. "Mom," I said at one point during our discussions about dropping out, "just let me make my own mistakes."

It was decided that I would leave school following the first half of my junior year. In Vermont, the "school-leaving age"—the minimum age at which a person is allowed to quit compulsory secondary education without a state-approved alternative plan—is sixteen. I turned sixteen on November 23, and my parents' only real request was that I finish out that term, which ran until the Christmas break. I agreed, and spent the next four weeks cutting as many classes as possible.

You'd think I would remember more about my last day of school, but I do not. I suspect I was excited, and probably more than a little nervous. I didn't have any grand ambitions; I knew I would have to find work, that I was not about to embark on an extended vacation. I possessed a modest amount of construction experience, which is to say, I had a basic understanding of how a hammer works and intimate knowledge regarding the pushing of brooms. Beyond this, I did not think about how my life might unfold, and while I am not entirely comfortable recommending that others emulate this path, I am often struck by the extent to which not adhering to rigid planning has freed me to live as I want to live *now*, rather than living in a manner intended to serve my assumed future interests.

The only thing I remember clearly from that day is coming down off the long hill next to the school. I was in my Rabbit, and as was my custom, I was driving too fast. It was cold, but I rolled down the window anyway to let the car fill with the December air. I passed no one, but if I had, they would have heard my still-deepening adolescent voice belting out the lyrics to my favorite song. "You control who I see . . . on Mondays." "Not anymore," I was thinking. "Not anymore."

There came a period after dropping out of school when I was neither man nor boy. I was living with my parents and, as anticipated, performing a variety of menial duties as the lowest man-boy on the totem pole of a small construction outfit. I believe I was making eight dollars per hour, but I can't be sure; it might have been a bit less or a bit more. I was not directionless exactly, but I was living less by design than by the slow accumulation of days.

In the spring after leaving school, I was involved in a freakish accident, whereby my best friend, Trevor, and I ran our cars headlong into each other. He was on his way to visit me, and I to visit him; unfortunately, we met somewhere in the middle, in a dramatic manner that left both of us stunned and speechless, with the exception of the two words we repeated over and over and over as we stood next to our crumpled-together vehicles (for the record, those two words were *holy* and *shit*). Neither of us was injured, but my car was severely damaged and never ran properly again. To replace it, I bought an old Cadillac for two hundred dollars. Almost immediately the head gasket blew, and I had to pull over every dozen miles or so to let it cool down and dump water into the radiator. To complicate matters, the alternator didn't work, so every night, when I got home from pushing brooms, I had to put the battery on a charger. Then one day I forgot to refill the radiator and the engine seized.

I junked the Caddy and picked up a Volkswagen Beetle for seventy-five dollars. The fuel pump was blown, so I mounted a gas can in the backseat, and ran a gravity feed to the carburetor. The foot brakes didn't work, but the emergency brake did, and I drove it like this—reeking of gas, reluctant to stop—for nearly two years without incident.

I took the Beetle to Martha's Vineyard, stopping every hundred miles or so to fill my makeshift backseat gas tank. On the Vineyard, I moved into a one-bedroom apartment with three friends. I got the couch and a job roofing for a fellow named Ken. Ken specialized in asphalt shingles, and we worked ten-hour days in the heat of July, wearing only socks, because shoes damaged the half-melted shingles. Ken also specialized in the consumption of high-grade marijuana, but rather than relax him, the weed seemed to make him explosive. Or maybe he would have been even more explosive without the pot, but whatever the case, he was always screaming at me. Plus, my feet hurt. So I quit.

Another contractor took me on. This was a better gig, because he specialized in authentic period restorations of large estate homes. Trevor (the same friend I'd crashed my Rabbit into back in Vermont) worked for him also, and we fell into a schedule that saw us begin work at six A.M., so that we might knock off by two or three. I bought a motorcycle, and in the afternoons, I took long rides on it or on my bicycle. I was only nineteen, but no longer drawn to recklessness. I worked hard and saved my money, although I wasn't sure what for.

One morning in early February, a woman arrived on the grounds of the estate where Trevor and I were working. It was an inhospitable day, not just drizzling but raining in earnest, and the temperature was in the mid-thirties. I remember hoping it might become cold enough that the rain would turn to snow. I'd grown accustomed to the distant ocean views from the upstairs windows of the house; I'd look out these windows often, grateful for the reprieve those views offered. On this day, I could not see the ocean, but I kept looking anyway, hoping to catch the transition from rain to snow.

That's how I knew the woman had arrived. She was riding a bicycle, bundled against the weather, and along the frame of her bicycle, she had strapped a pickax and a shovel. It was barely seven A.M., and the woman I would soon come to learn was named Penny had ridden her bike through the rain-verging-on-snow so that she could spend the day in the rain-verging-on-snow, digging a trench for the estate's new sprinkler system. To say a woman who would do such a thing intrigued me is an understatement of epic proportions, and although I was the sort of young man who as a rule could not summon the courage to do such things, I soon asked her out.

Around the time Penny came into my life, I also began writing. On my days off, I'd wake up early to fill notebooks with stories and small observations, some invented, some drawn directly from my days. At the time, I did not see the parallel between my nascent writing habit and my grade-school reading routine. But I do now.

I had no idea that writing would or even could become a source of income and, eventually, the primary means by which I would support my family. I wrote for the same reasons my sons carve bows or boil maple syrup: because there was something in it that whispered to me, that fed some part of me that could not be fed otherwise. No one told me I had to write or even that I should write. Likewise, no one told me I shouldn't or couldn't write, or what I could or should write about.

The self-motivated nature of my writing practice makes a comparison to my sons' learning all but inevitable. I sometimes wonder if I'd have the same confidence in Fin and Rye's ability to direct their learning if it weren't for my writing, because it was through my self-directed pursuit of it that I learned to have similar confidence in myself. Clearly, there were influences that helped me cultivate that confidence. My father wrote poetry, my mother wrote children's books, and for a large swath of my childhood, there was no television in the house. There were all those predawn hours spent reading, escaping into stories in which I was not an overweight, unpopular child. And truncated as it was, my high school education did include a handful of writing classes, the brief periods of my schooling in which I felt as if I actually belonged. But it wasn't until I'd left high school that I truly began to understand what writing could do for me. What *I* could do for *myself*.

The funny thing is, I strongly suspect that if I hadn't dropped out of high school, I'd never have discovered writing as a profession. In dropping out, I had by default shifted the trajectory of my education in a way that was not likely to include college-level learning (after earning my GED, I did complete two semesters in the Vermont state college system), and therefore freed me of the financial burden such learning would have placed upon me, to say nothing of whatever expectations might have evolved in the process. Certainly, college was the presumed outcome for me. My father had earned his undergraduate degree at Cornell and his master's at Johns Hopkins; my mother had graduated from Iowa's Grinnell

College. In a delicious bit of irony, at the time of my dropping out, my father actually worked for the Vermont Department of Education. Mine was a family that didn't merely believe in structured education; we were fed and sheltered by it.

The transition from writing as a hobby to writing as a profession was not rapid. For many years, I continued earning a living by alternately working construction and repairing bicycles, all the while amassing a collection of published stories in minor periodicals. This continued until I awakened to the dawning realization that maybe, just maybe, I could support myself full-time through my writing.

Every so often, I allow myself the indulgence of imagining my sons' future. I have no right to such imaginings, although so long as I do not allow my imagination to become a breeding ground for expectation, I suspect it's a fairly harmless indulgence. For their part, the boys seem rather certain of what the world holds for them. Not so long ago, I overheard Fin and Rye talking, and there was something in their tone that made me listen more carefully than I might have otherwise, an earnestness suggesting that matters of great and lasting importance were being discussed.

"Rye, if you could have any three things in the world, what would they be?"

My eight-year-old younger son did not hesitate for even a moment:

"Traps, a donkey, and a cabin," he replied emphatically, and at that moment, I felt a small ache. Part of it was happiness, the recognition that a boy can still be drawn to such things in a world that has all but forgotten they exist. But there was sadness, too, because I knew how unusual my sons' three wishes were. "What will the world do with a boy who grows up wanting traps, a donkey, and cabin?" I thought. And then: "What will a boy who grows up wanting traps, a donkey, and a cabin do with the world?" When I expressed these concerns to Penny, she paused for a moment before replying. "Well," she said, "it's probably a lot more realistic than growing up wanting to play third base for the Red Sox."

Like all parents, I must live with this uncertainty, although I suspect my sons' unique interests exacerbate it. *Traps, a donkey, and a cabin.* Penny and I do not have the comfort of our children sharing the commonplace interests of their peers. But we are not comfortless, because every day we observe their resourcefulness and adaptability as they go about their self-directed tasks. Every day, we see them transform the unknown into the known, and we witness the constellation of experience, success, failure, and satisfaction that results from their learning.

Every time I consider the boys' futures, I remind myself of this. And I remind myself of my own journey, and how I have come to understand that even events most would consider limiting became opportunities. Not opportunities in the way our culture has come to think of opportunities, as being about advancement and recognition, but opportunities in terms of illuminating a different path. Maybe the boys really will live together in a cabin, eking out a small living from the land, riding their donkeys into town on the full moon of every third month for supplies. Maybe, like the old woodsman we recently read about, they will allow so much time to lapse between changing clothes that their body hair will grow into and eventually through their long underwear. "That's how I want to be!" Fin chortled, when he heard the tale. Or maybe they'll become doctors, or bankers, or something that defies such easy categorization.

The truth is there are so many permutations of what it means to live a good life, and I often wonder if all I really want for my children is the ability to determine which permutation is right for them.

HELD

In the middle of August, after he's taken the second cutting of hay off the hilltop field that borders the long row of maples towering over our shared fence line, Melvin turns his milkers loose to graze whatever fringes the mower missed. At four thirty every afternoon, my boys duck under the fence and step onto Melvin's hayfield to drive the cows down for evening milking. It's a quarter mile or more to the barn, down the steep hill that not so long ago was home to a ski tow Melvin's sons had rigged up by suspending the front end of an old car at the hill's crest and wrapping the tow rope around one of the drive wheels.

The boys covet this task. Fin and Rye have reached the age at which they are eager to prove they are growing into the young men they will become, and there is perhaps no better proof of such a thing than successfully driving a herd of thirty milk cows across a high, green hayfield and down into the barnyard below. Perhaps, like me, they recognize that at sixty-five, Melvin is approaching the end of his milking days and they can sense that some year in the not-too-distant future, it is likely there won't be any cows to drive to the barn for evening milking. Still, I suspect that's not much of a factor; they're only eleven and eight, after all. They're too young to be motivated by sentiment.

I, however, am not, and so one late-summer evening around six I traced the boys' path to the barn, ostensibly to relay to Melvin my sons' account of how one of his cows had spooked during that afternoon's roundup and pushed through a weak section of fence. But a phone call would have sufficed, and the real reason for my walk (although I couldn't admit it to myself at the time) was no more complicated than the simple fact that I know it won't be many more summers before I won't have such a ready excuse to stroll across that field. I won't have such a ready excuse to tromp down the meandering path cut into the hillside by the force of literally hundreds of thousands of hoofprints over all the years Melvin's cows have shuffled their unhurried way up and down that slope. I won't have such a ready excuse to stand in our neighbor's barnyard, him on one side of a windowless window frame and me on the other, chatting about the weather and haying and pasture and all the meaningless minutia of our day. Meaningless to anyone but us, that is.

Living between two dairy farms has proven to be one of the greatest unanticipated and unplanned blessings of our existence on this hill. We did not buy this property with such a thing in mind; we would not even have known to look for such a thing. And yet now I can't even imagine anything else, and I find it literally impossible to express the ways in which it has enriched our lives, perhaps because some of these ways defy logic or reason.

I don't like to think of Melvin's inevitable retirement, although of course I want what's best for him. But when I see Fin and Rye coming back from herding the cows down to evening milking, walking along the hayfield's ridge, nothing visible behind them but sky, as if one false step would send them plummeting off the edge of the world, I just want time to stop. When I stand in on one side of that windowless window frame with Melvin leaning against the other side, the late-day sun washing us both, and behind him the soft outlines of his cows as they stand for milking, I want time to stop. I want time to stop because in these moments, I am certain of the rightness of the world and of how I fit into it. I am certain that everything I need—have ever needed, am likely ever to need— is within my reach.

But here's the thing about time: It keeps on going. Kids grow up, dairy farmers retire, a hayfield turns to forest and then back to hayfield. Things change, both in ways that can be anticipated and in those that can't. Someday, Melvin will stop farming. Someday, my children will no longer herd his cows, either because he no longer has cows or because they are no longer interested. Either will be difficult for me to witness, and yet given the passage of enough time, both are inevitable. It is only a question of which comes first.

In my life I have seen, time and time again, how things that were once within my reach move beyond it. I think about the people I have cared for who have died or simply moved or drifted away. I think about the passing phases of my children, how Fin no longer wants to hold hands the way he used to, how I can no longer hoist either of them atop my shoulders at will. I try to remember the final hand hold, the final shoulder ride. But I cannot.

Likewise, I have seen how things I could never have imagined needing have become things I can hardly imagine doing without, and to live with the knowledge of their eventual departure is to live in harmony with the grief their leaving will impart. Sometimes I think of these things as birds landing on a branch. They perch for a while and then, for reasons known only to them, take flight again.

Occasionally, I am visited by a sense of nostalgia, not for an earlier era or for some past event but for the future nostalgia I know I will feel for now. I suspect that is what I'm feeling in those moments I want time to stop: the storage of the present experience for a future recalling. My boys, etched against the sky. My neighbor, framed by the window opening of his dilapidated barn. The cow-worn path, hard and rutted under my feet.

I know it is not merely my memory that is absorbing these small moments. It is my emotional core. It is my character. It is my spirit. It is everything that makes me me, and in the flickering seconds when I feel the influence of these moments on the very core of how I think and feel and perceive the world around me, I have this sense of being held in the palm of this place. Of here and now.

5

The Early Years

I OFFERED THE PREVIOUS CHAPTER's incomplete history of my formal education because I have little doubt that it contains the foundation stones—or at least some of them—of our decision to educate Fin and Rye at home. Of course, Penny had plenty to say about this decision, and if anything, her resolve has been stronger than mine, despite having come closer than I to walking the prescribed middle-class American educational path of high school and four years of higher education. Indeed, she came remarkably near to fulfilling this expectation at the Rochester Institute of Technology, where she pursued a degree in photography. Then came a summer spent working on a vegetable farm and with it the realization that a row of carrots held more fascination for her than a roll of film. Penny was not the first almost-college graduate to be derailed by seeds and soil, and she certainly won't be the last.

Or maybe her unwavering commitment to keep Fin and Rye out of mainstream schooling institutions was not founded *despite* being immersed in contemporary educational convention but precisely *because* of this immersion and the recognition of its hollow rewards. Certainly, this commitment was forged in part by circumstance. Early in our relationship, I'd returned to Vermont for a summer, while Penny stayed in Martha's Vineyard to work on the vegetable farm where she'd spent most of her days since leaving RIT.

Serendipitously, through a series of word-of-mouth connections,

I rented a bunkhouse attached to a rambling homestead known locally as "Resurrection City," or "Camp RC" for short. Resurrection from what, and toward what end, I never determined, and it didn't matter to me anyway. I wasn't looking for renewal, just a cheap place to lay my head, and at seventy-five dollars per month, Camp RC qualified. Other than me, the primary tenant was a thirty-something fellow named Donald, who lived with his two young sons, Crescent and Orion. I don't remember precisely how old the boys were during my bunkhouse tenure—I'm guessing somewhere in the five-to-eight-year-old range—but I do remember that neither of them attended school. Instead, they stayed home with Donald, playing and exploring and accompanying him wherever he went.

Donald always seemed to find work that made this possible. In the spring, he made maple syrup at a neighboring farm while Crescent and Orion played in the snow or skied laps around the sugarhouse. He took small carpentry jobs and, provoked by either desperation or inspiration (and possibly, some combination of the two) started a mobile burrito kitchen. The three of them hawked vegetarian burritos at festivals and concerts and pretty much anywhere Donald—who had an uncanny ability to ferret out this sort of information—determined there would be a sufficient quantity of burrito eaters willing to part with their hard-earned money.

I don't know if Crescent and Orion were homeschooled or unschooled, or some combination of the two that's not so readily defined, but I do know that they were unusual children. They had few toys, and seemed entirely unaware of this dearth, perhaps because to them, everything was a toy. Everything was a game. I vividly remember them playing for hours with two discarded lengths of metal pipe, pretending they were canes, then fishing poles, then crutches. They would have been no more satisfied with the most elaborate set of Legos money can buy.

More so than other young children I'd met up to that point, they possessed a sense of self and a unique degree of confidence and awareness that eluded most adults I knew. They were precocious—mischievous, even—but even that was charming, if only because their antics were those of children engaged with their world. There was an unguarded childlike quality to Crescent and Orion, and I realize how silly that might sound: they were *children*, after all. But watching them play and scamper and tussle, I was struck by the extent to which most children I'd known in my young life simply weren't allowed such freedom of expression.

Whether this was because of a deficit of time and space or of simple patience and tolerance, I wasn't sure. I was only sure—as was Penny, when she came for a visit and met the boys—that my small friends knew a degree of happiness and freedom that I would want for my children, if ever I had them. Penny had been the favored babysitter of her suburban neighborhood and as such was familiar with the variable characteristics of young children. But Crescent and Orion were originals. "I've never met kids like them," she said. "They're amazing."

It would add a degree of drama to my story to suggest that we wrestled with a multitude of options regarding our sons' education, but from the moment we met Crescent and Orion, we knew: if we had children, they would be schooled at home. True, we did not know precisely how that learning would unfold, or how our days would be structured. But we knew, with a confidence that belied our inexperience as both parents and educators, that our boys would not attend school. Such certainty is arguably naive and maybe even a little bit arrogant; after all, we're talking about unborn children. To pretend to know what will be best for them a half-dozen and more years hence demands no small amount of hubris. But of course the same could be said of any assumptions regarding our children's future, and perhaps there is no less hubris in our collective faith that a more formal educational path is the one our children should walk.

Despite not knowing the exacting details of how we would educate our children, Penny and I knew that we wanted to retain the ability to guide their learning in ways that would largely be lost to us if they attended school. Which is to say, we wanted them to have *less* guidance than school would provide; we wanted them to experience a degree of freedom and simple playfulness that is increasingly imperiled in modern America. In short, we wanted our kids to be *kids,* to develop and learn at their own pace, and in their own style. We had felt, acutely, the suffocating sense of having a standardized education thrust upon us, and we wanted something entirely different for our children. We did not want them to suffocate; we wanted them to *breathe,* and we did not believe they could breathe unless we reclaimed those thousands upon thousands of hours they'd otherwise pass in school.

Still, our journey to committed unschooling began haltingly. Our early efforts at home education were modeled in part on the Waldorf style of teaching. Waldorf is based on the educational beliefs of Rudolf Steiner, the Austrian philosopher and founder of anthroposophy, which postulates the existence of an intellectually comprehensible spiritual world. According to Steiner, this world is accessible to anyone willing to cultivate deep perception and intuition. Waldorf is the largest so-called alternative-education movement in the world, with more than a thousand established private schools in sixty countries.

The Waldorf philosophy appealed to us primarily because it emphasizes the importance of teaching basic skills via art, crafts, and other expressive activities. In short, the belief that all the rote information our sons would need to know—reading, writing, arithmetic, and so on—are best learned in the context of a child's artistic pursuits.

This sounded swell to Penny and me, and so when Fin reached five, the age at which we deemed it necessary to introduce some structure into his learning, Penny established a schedule around their daily art-and-crafts endeavors. She set up a station at the kitchen table, which bowed under heavy reams of thick art paper, along with an expansive range of watercolors and pastels. It was a beautiful sight, particularly when the morning sun broke over the horizon and brushed everything with its honeyed light. It just looked so . . . nurturing.

There was just one problem: Fin wasn't the least bit on board.

He'd never so much as heard of Rudolph Steiner; he didn't know he was supposed to love sitting and expressing himself artistically.

In short, Fin *hated* it. He'd never been a particularly docile child, and the expectation that he would sit at that table quietly expressing himself through his art unleashed something close to fury in him. He fought every second of it. He bucked and keened and wailed. He fidgeted and fussed. He didn't want to sit at that table for even a minute; indeed, he didn't really want to sit anywhere at all. "What the hell would a Waldorf school do with this kid?" Penny remarked after one particularly exasperating session that had ended in tears for all involved.

Penny's question was rhetorical, because even if we could have afforded the tuition, we had no intention of sending our son to a Waldorf school, and this was particularly true once we came to understand and accept that Fin's temperament simply wasn't suited to sit-down learning. He'd always been a child-in-motion, one of those kids for whom silence and stillness are anathema. For all his childhood, there was precisely one time he napped of his own accord; every other midday snooze was a hard-fought affair, coming only after being in the car, or a walk through the woods, with him folded into a sling, his eyes covered simply so he'd stop looking around. So he'd stop engaging for long enough to provide him (and us) some much-needed rest.

I have no doubt that if Fin had been sent to a public school, he would have been diagnosed with Attention Deficit Hyperactivity Disorder (ADHD) and summarily prescribed behavior-modifying drugs. Indeed, were we not inclined to allow our children to learn at home, anyway, the simple fact of Fin's temperament and the threat of such a diagnosis would have compelled us to keep him out of school. The sad fact is that drugs like Adderall and Ritalin, which so profoundly alter the neural pathways in the brain as to be addictive, have become a de rigueur part of our nation's public education system. In 2010, sales of these drugs surpassed the seven-billion-dollar mark, an increase of 83 percent over just four years,[1] and by 2013, 11 percent of school-aged children would be diagnosed with some form of attention deficiency.

The acceptance of who our son was rather than who we thought he should be marked a crucial turning point in Penny's and my journey of unlearning the expectations and assumptions we'd been socialized to. I now view our son's high-octane temperament as being one of the great blessings of our lives, for if he had been an easygoing child, willing to apply himself to whatever lessons we placed before him, we might never have allowed ourselves to grant our children the freedom that has been so essential to their growth and development. We might never have granted ourselves the freedom that has been so essential to our growth and development.

Once we abandoned the notion that Fin should learn in any particular style, it was as if a blindfold had been torn from our eyes. No longer were we mired in concept; now, we could observe. And what we observed was that the son we worried would never be able to quiet his body and mind enough to concentrate on a particular task was actually capable of tremendous focus. Liberated from paint, paper, and all assumptions about how he should learn, Fin immersed himself in projects that seemed to blossom from some primal place deep inside him. At first, these projects had no discernible end: He spent hours hammering nails into a single piece of wood, or whittling a stick until it was so thin it splintered in his hand. But gradually, his pursuits became tangible. He built bows, spending hours carving and sanding. He became an expert at making cordage from gossamer threads of cedar bark. He fished for hours at a time, seemingly unconcerned by the dearth of fish he brought home. He learned to kindle fire from flint and steel, to identify the trees and plants in our forest. So determined was he to make a pack basket that he spent an entire day weaving splints into shape, and by seven the next morning he was back at it.

Of course, he did not teach himself all of these skills; liberating our son from our preconceived notions regarding what his education should look like did not uncap a deep reservoir of knowledge and experience that had been lying in wait for the very moment of our enlightenment. Nor were the majority of these skills handed down from Penny and me, who could no sooner have taught him to make cordage than to construct a nuclear reactor. Instead, we sought ways to connect Fin with other adults experienced in working with children in the natural world. We visited a nature program for kids, but quickly realized that the overstimulation of so many peers was not a good match for Fin's temperament, so we hired one of the instructors to work with our son one-on-one.

The instructor's name was Erik, and every week he came to our home, whereupon he and Fin would disappear into the woods for hours. Later, when Fin turned eight and it was clear he was ready for the stimulation of a group, we signed him up for a one-day-per-week wilderness-skills program. He flourished there, returning each Thursday afternoon glowing from the day's excitement and, I suspect, the sense of having found a place where he felt as if he belonged. Today, Fin is still part of this group, and Erik still comes to our house every week. But now, it is Rye he accompanies into the woods.

Rye's temperament is so different from Fin's that had he come first, we might have gone farther down the path of a more structured homeschooling regimen. Rye shares Penny's organizational tendencies, and is in general a quieter, more introspective child. I do not think he would thrive under the onus of a structured curriculum, be it at home or in school, but I do think he would at least survive. Fortunately for us all, Fin showed us a different path.

A question I ask myself with some frequency, and particularly as I struggle with one or another of our parenting choices is this: "What is an education?" And, not inconsequently, "What is a childhood? Should it be one thing, and not another?" It's a silly question, really, a bit like asking, "What is a person? Should she be one thing and not another?" But even if it is silly, it grounds me. It reminds me that the assumptions we have arrived at regarding education are just that: assumptions. They are stories born of a culture, and like all stories, we can choose to believe them or not. We can choose to listen or not. We can choose, even, to write our own stories.

Part of the story I am attempting to write with my children is the story of trust. Of letting go and trusting my instincts as a parent, which is a luxury I can allow myself only if I can learn to have trust in my boys. Simple trust, the confidence in our children and in ourselves to allow them to unfold at their own pace. The confidence that they *will* unfold, even when it seems as if they are falling behind the manufactured expectations set by institutionalized schooling.

Not so long ago, when Rye was seven, I mentioned to someone that he did not yet read. She was shocked, and not only because my son couldn't read but, I believe, because I was so unconcerned. "Really?" she kept asking. *"Really?"* As if this were some unconquerable failing that would haunt him all his life. I was not offended. I know what the expectations are, what they have become. I know that by age seven, my children are expected to be reading, to be multiplying endless rows of numbers across a page, to be sitting for hours on end, bent over pencil and paper or, as is increasingly likely, a laptop or iPad. I know what they're expected to know, and often, in this regard, I recognize how my children fall short.

Yet it is what Fin and Rye are *not* expected to know that is so fascinating to me. To identify every tree in our woodlot. To butcher a hog. To wield a splitting maul and use a chop saw. To make a fire. To know when a windrow of hay is dry enough for baling. To build a cabin. To sew and knit and carve. To disappear into the woods below our home and return an hour later with a bag full of chanterelle and hedgehog mushrooms. To operate Melvin's bale wrapper, so they can help him during the crush of summer. These skills feel important to me because they are the skills of a particular place, having arisen from their connection to this land and community. And they feel important because they are true life skills. They are instilling in my boys a degree of hands-on resourcefulness that is rapidly being lost in a society where many people do not even know how to change a tire, or hold an ax. Finally, I see how the skills and the knowledge they embody are the direct result of my sons' innate curiosities and love of learning. To be sure, their exposure to the particulars of this place has played a role in defining the subjects their love of learning has landed upon. Such a thing is unavoidable.

But none of it has been forced. None of it has come attached to reward or acclaim beyond the quiet satisfaction inherent in the process of learning and the completion of a task. Penny and I believe in presence, not praise. We are here to support and facilitate, but not to cajole and manipulate, through either threat or incentive. The boys' unhampered curiosity is incentive enough. The learning is its own reward.

Can the same be said of schooled learning? Of course it can. Loving to learn and being compelled to learn from a prescribed curriculum are not mutually exclusive. But there is little question that the overwhelming majority of institutionalized learning occurs in isolation from the tangible realities of place and form, of how the world feels and looks, tastes and smells and sounds. I believe it is crucial for children to learn in ways that are not held in isolation, that involve the body as well as the mind, and that result in something real and tangible. Even better, something of service: a shelter where once there was none; food in a freezer that was previously empty; or even just a piece of clothing mended by their own hands. Interestingly, this is precisely the sort of learning that is rapidly disappearing from public education in the wake of diminishing budgets and immersion in the abstraction of technology.

I have seen how even a child's whim or want of a frivolity can provide an opportunity for them to create something real. When Fin was five, he desired nothing in this world so much as a popgun. For weeks, we put him off, his pleas growing more ardent by the day. It wasn't that we didn't want him to have a popgun, but rather that we didn't want to buy him a plastic bauble that would in short order be reduced to landfill. So Penny set about researching how to make a popgun, slowly gathering the materials in anticipation of a teachable mother-son project. "He's going to love this," she told me once she'd finally settled on a design.

The next morning, before Penny could astound our son with her ingenuity and resourcefulness, something curious happened: Fin careened into the house with a contraption in his hands. "Look what I made!" he hollered, waving in our faces the popgun he'd designed and summarily constructed. Penny and I were mute with surprise. Without so much as consulting us or even watching a YouTube video on the subject, our five-year-old son had designed and built a popgun. What's more, the darn thing actually worked. Sure, it was simple, little more than a length of copper pipe fitted with a dowel of appropriate diameter that slammed into the cork he'd shaved until it could be squeezed into the pipe's end. But simple or not, it worked. The cork flew.

How many times, I wondered, have we profoundly underestimated our children's abilities? How many times have we simply given them what they've asked for, in the process short-circuiting their sense of discovery, their ability to imagine and create, to fail and succeed? It happens less often now than it once did, but still I suspect it has been an awful lot, and I am reminded of a friend's comment that her young children's "art" class in school consisted primarily of coloring inside prescribed outlines. "They don't leave much room for imagination," she said, and I flinched at the comment, because of course imagination is what we should be leaving the *most* room for.

The danger in "color between the lines" learning is the degree to which it conditions children to need direction. As adults, few of us even recognize this because of course we too have been conditioned to the need for direction. Witnessing Fin and Rye construct innumerable implements of their devising has revealed to Penny and me the glaring lack of our own resourcefulness. Like most people in our society, we were taught to need instruction.

One could argue that the knowledge we hope to imbue in our sons is not mutually exclusive to a conventional schooling experience. This is true. But another truth is that any child, like any adult, has only so many waking hours in a day, and if those hours are passed inside the four walls of a classroom, or gazing into a pixilated screen, they are by default not spent otherwise. If a child is spending seven or eight hours in a classroom each day, plus another two or three (or more) hours completing homework assignments, plus whatever other extracurricular activities are on his or her plate, plus however much time he or she spends commuting to school, plus whatever time is devoted to television and other passive entertainment mediums, there simply isn't any time remaining to develop relationships outside the context of these institutions.

Every so often, I fall victim to the manufactured educational expectations of our culture, and I worry that my boys will remain forever out of step with twenty-first-century America. Could Penny and I be condemning them to a life of toil and meager wages, bereft of the information they need to land the sort of job parents are supposed to want for their children? Is it possible that by not introducing them to Facebook, or by not equipping them with smart phones and iPads, or by not compelling them to sit for hours on end memorizing multiplication tables and textbook history lessons, we are disadvantaging them? In these moments, I fret over the many things they don't know, and think, "My God, am I failing them?" Or I consider my own unlikely education, and my still-bloated ignorance and all the times it feels as if I know nothing or, if not nothing, then not enough.

Of course, I cannot know with any real certainty that I am not failing my children. This is the cross all parents must bear: *We cannot know.* We cannot know what their future will be, if they will end up as bankers or boatbuilders, lawyers or linesmen, doctors or ditch-diggers. We cannot know if they will be happy and contented, or bitter and maladjusted. We cannot know the state of the world they will inhabit. If everything goes according to plan, we will die before their journey is anywhere near to being over and we will know even less. One of the most important jobs I have as a parent—and perhaps simply as a human—is to learn how to peacefully coexist with this uncertainty.

One might accurately note that completing high school and even college does not preclude happiness and contentment. But that's not what I'm suggesting. Rather, I'm suggesting, based on personal experience, that living a good and meaningful life is not dependent on walking our culture's prescribed educational path. That may sound painfully, if not insultingly, obvious. Yet our society seems to have attached itself to the notion that institutional, standardized education is *precisely* the path our children must walk if they are to thrive in this world. Perhaps this is correct, although it's interesting to note that homeschoolers graduate college at a higher rate than their peers—66.7 percent compared to 57.5 percent. Not only that, but they earn higher grade-point averages than their schooled classmates along the way.[2]

It seems to me as if most educational institutions view it as their duty to prepare children for the economy as it exists, with all its inherent assumptions regarding happiness and prosperity. And really, who can blame them? After all, this is precisely what we demand of them: give our children the skills necessary to succeed in the context of the socioeconomic arrangements upon which we have all come to depend. The problem is, we demand this without seriously considering whether or not these arrangements create a world we all want to inhabit. So long as these institutions groom our children to compete and excel on a global stage, in an economy that reveres growth and defines success and security in terms of money and force, a world of true peace and equality will remain achingly out of reach. In short, the feedback loops built into our contemporary economy will not be overcome so long as we continue to educate our youth in a manner that upholds them.

In my own life, and with the benefit of a quarter century of hindsight, I now see that leaving high school was actually an enabling factor. Not so much for the doors it opened and the so-called opportunities it presented, but for having played a role in changing my view of what mattered. For having freed me to make my own way in this world, before I had so much invested—materially, emotionally, physically—in a more traditional path that I might never have dared deviate from. Our society carries strong assumptions about what constitutes a successful life and about the sort of person that becomes a high school dropout. Or the sort a person a high school dropout becomes.

In fairness, statistics do play a role in developing these assumptions. After all, among dropouts between the ages of sixteen and twenty-four, incarceration rates were *sixty-three times* higher than those of college graduates.[3] But of course correlation is not causation, and it seems reasonable to wonder if this correlation is less the result of some inherent "badness" associated with dropping out of school and more the result of the stigma we attach to leaving school, and the lack of support provided to those who do not follow through with a formal education. It seems fair to wonder: if more children were allowed to pursue their own paths outside of school, free of judgment and supported by their communities, might they find ways to bring meaningful and positive contributions to this world?

It is so easy to explain and demonstrate success in the context of our culture's common vernacular regarding achievement. Home ownership, a good-paying job, a generous 401(k), a nice car, recognition, personal ambition to achieve these things: These are some of the metrics by which our culture has come to define success, and because they are commonly understood to be so, they have become a sort of shorthand for a life well lived. Or perhaps it is simply a life of comfort, which itself seems to serve as an emblem of a life well lived.

It is not that there's anything particularly wrong with any of these metrics in isolation. These are not inherently bad things, and indeed, I have some of them myself. The danger is that the pursuit of them threatens to hijack our lives in ways that make it difficult for us to cultivate meaningful relationships with place and nature. The problem is that we pursue them—both for ourselves and on behalf of our children—without considering the ramifications of our pursuit, how it can pull us away from one another, how it can fragment family and community, how the attempt to ensure our economic success can sacrifice our freedom. And how this pursuit can do the same thing to our children.

Penny and I have not made the choices we have—around education, money, ambition, and so on—because we think we are going to heal the world. We are not that foolish, nor that virtuous. But while these choices may not immediately influence the trajectory of global affairs, they are ultimately a reflection of the world we wish to inhabit, and in that sense, they become the world we wish to inhabit. It is a world in which children feel trusted, useful, and respected, where generosity is stronger than greed, and where all people are liberated to live in a manner that affords them the freedom to be generous and trusting. It is a world in which it is commonly understood that all the seemingly overwhelming forces of humankind, many of which cause hardship and despair, depend on us to feel dependent on them. They depend on us not realizing that with every choice we make, with every action we take, we are shaping the world. Our world.

THEN I WALKED HOME

Summer comes as summer does, fast and undeniable, bringing with it the means to fill each of its days, from their gauzy five A.M. beginnings to the exhausted, body-sore collapse into sleep. There is firewood to be cut, split, and stacked; a woodshed to be built for the firewood to be stacked into; a stand of mature fir to be thinned, skidded, and sawn. Then there are the boards, redolent of the earthy sweetness of fresh-cut lumber, to be stickered and covered. Fence posts to be set; the raspberries to be thinned and trellised; dozens of vegetable beds to be broadforked, weeded, and seeded. The sheep and pigs and cows to be turned out to pasture. Hay to be baled; bales to be loaded, thrown, stacked. And then the cows freshen and there is suddenly milk everywhere and even better, cream: To turn to butter, to cut the bitterness of strong coffee, to whip, to slurp by the cupful straight from a quart jar while standing before the open fridge in chainsaw chaps and a sweat-damp T-shirt. Fishing trips with the boys, walking downhill through the woods to the neighbor's stream, where the brookies hide in the shadows of a tumble-down stone bridge, half or more fallen in, uncrossed for decades and perhaps even generations.

One morning I awoke particularly early, for Rye's cat, Winslow, had squeezed his way through the gate through which he is not supposed to squeeze and pranced his way upstairs, where he settled into a spot directly to the right of my slumbering head and commenced to purr maliciously. It was 4:45 A.M., or thereabouts, so I shuffled downstairs to make a cup of coffee, and then, just as soon as I thought perhaps I could make out the shaggy forms of the sheep in the murky half-light of predawn beyond the kitchen window, I strolled outside.

It was eerie warm, the air soup-thick and rank with the smell of the skunks the boys had trapped the day prior for our friend Todd. Not for the first time (and certainly not for the last), I cursed my sons' odd desires and also Penny's and my willingness to accommodate them. I mean, really: Who in their right mind would let their children trap skunks and skin them in the front yard? Who in their right mind would let their children build a trapping shed at the junction of lawn and driveway, in plain smell of the house? I want to support my boys and all, but sometimes it just seems like it'd be a hell of a lot easier if they were into Xbox and Little League. Sometimes, it just seems like it'd be a hell of a lot easier if we just said no a little more often.

I spent the remainder of the early morning moving from animal to animal as the sky went about its business of exchanging dark for light. Pigs, chickens, and the new batch of piglets, down in the nascent nut grove, rutting out the wild raspberries and spreading their rich manure. I strolled down to the cows at the far end of the pasture, and stood under the big apple tree along Melvin's boundary and ours, just watching. I'd had the idea I might gather some wind-dropped fruit for the pigs, but I'd brought no bucket and hadn't even worn a shirt from which to fashion a carrier, and I realized how foolish I'd been.

A minute passed, maybe two. It was not raining, but it felt as if might start, and I remembered the ending lines of Hayden Carruth's poem "The Cows at Night":

But I did not want to go,
not yet, nor knew what to do
if I should stay, for how

in that great darkness could I explain
anything, anything at all.
I stood by the fence. And then

very gently it began to rain.

Then I walked home.

6

Big Sticks

On January 14, 2002, in the chaotic, dust-thick midst of a house that had no kitchen sink, finished floors, exterior siding, or drywall, Penny went into labor with our first child. She was grocery shopping when the unmistakable grip of contractions began, and she continued filling her basket as our Finlay made his imminence known. Befitting my wife's pragmatic nature, she crossed each and every item off her list and then, having coolly calculated the pace of contractions to achieve a rough estimation of her allotted time before things got down to business, continued on to the lumberyard, where she loaded a dozen boxes of slate shower tiles into the trunk of our car before embarking on the twenty-five-mile drive home. Upon arrival, Penny settled into our bedroom (which is to say, there was a bare, unfinished room with a mattress on the floor, so we called it a "bedroom") and I called the midwife, Judy, before embarking on a frenzied quest to transform our construction zone into something more amenable to the birth of a child.

This was to be our midwife's first visit to our home; from our prenatal appointments, I had gotten the impression that she did not hold me in high regard. There was something disdainful in her manner whenever she addressed or responded to me, a haughtiness that suggested distaste for my company. I could only guess at the reasons for this distaste, which had uncharacteristically given me a desire to impress upon her that I was, in fact, a fine and upstanding young man, providing for my wife and child-to-be in a manner that spoke of responsibility, compassion, and general competence. Did the piles of debris and strewn-about, sharp-bladed tools with which we shared our living space evoke these qualities? I thought not, and so as Penny endured her deepening contractions in our little flophouse of a bedroom at the top of the stairs (which is to say, there was an ascending set of creaky rough plank treads, so we called them "stairs"), I busied myself humping the jagged-toothed cutting implements to the basement and consolidating the various piles of construction detritus.

Thirty minutes later, Judy swept into our home, casting her gaze around our rudimentary living quarters, which to my eyes had never looked more splendid. I'd even relocated the table saw to the basement, a process that normally required two able-bodied humans. The impending arrival of both our midwife and our child seemed to have imbued me with superhuman strength and catlike agility. "Well, you sure have a long way to go," Judy huffed as she swept into the house on a cloud of frigid air. She tromped up the wobbly stairs and settled into a rocking chair perched directly in the *center of the bedroom doorway.* There, she fell into a deep and restful slumber. In fairness, I am compelled to point out that Judy was an exceptionally experienced and highly regarded midwife, and we'd chosen her to help bring our first child into the world specifically because of these qualities. Still, for Rye's birth, we retained the services of a midwife whose competence was accompanied by kindness toward both me and our home.

This may sound sort of obvious, but there is something amazing about having your children born at home, into the protective shell of a house you have assembled from piles of bare lumber. How many boards had I nailed together over the prior year? How many trees had lost their lives to the home that was slowly taking shape around us, and into which my sons would emerge from their small, private oceans? I remember, with striking clarity, placing my hands under each of their warm, wet heads and feeling, with just that brief whisper of first contact, the sweet and infinite vulnerability of parenthood wash over me.

It's not that you can't experience these things at a hospital birth, of course, but every day I walk past the precise spots on the living room floor where my sons came into this world, the precise spots where I crouched atop those foot-worn boards to receive their tiny bodies, and hold them for a greedy second longer than absolutely necessary before placing them against Penny's chest.

Having children was, of course, a life-altering event, but unlike our land, which has imprinted itself upon us slowly and in a manner that occasionally leaves me second-guessing whether or not its influence is as absolute as I imagine, the force of children is both immediate and irrefutable. The impact is at once acute and emotionally fluid: Joy. Fear. Pride. Confusion. Worry. Joy again. More pride, more worry. Behind it all, the omnipresent sense that your life has ceased being yours and yours alone, because there is suddenly a person whose well-being matters more than your own, more than anything else in the world. You might never have thought such a thing possible, but even if you did, you find yourself nearly stricken by the sheer force and certainty of this truth.

Lacking as it may have been in many of the twenty-first century's assumed comforts, the house into which Fin and Rye were born was a distinct improvement over the humble cabin we'd begun assembling immediately after taking title to our land. The plans for this cabin had been sketched onto the back of an envelope by the small light of a candle and were open to a broad sweep of interpretation. Still, some things were known. For instance, we knew the cabin would measure sixteen feet by thirty-two feet, with a sleeping loft tucked under its roof. We knew the roof would be steeply angled so snow would slide off of its own accord, and we knew it would be metal so that we might fall asleep to the sound of rain on tin. And we knew the frame of the cabin would be built of large timbers procured from a local sawmill. "Mr. Hewitt, them are some big sticks," the mill's proprietor told me when I placed the order. For no particularly good reason, this pleased me. *Them are some big sticks.* Damn straight, fella.

We worked hastily, almost frantically, driven by our desire to extricate ourselves from the damp, moldy, cigarette-smoke-stained hovel we'd rented for the previous year and a half. One hundred bucks per month the place cost us, but of course that wasn't the full toll, because, put bluntly, the place was a turd, a dark and dispiriting burrow into which congeniality and general happiness could disappear, never to be seen again. It wasn't that we had to haul drinking water from our respective work places; it wasn't that the roof leaked, or that the bathroom consisted of a dilapidated and poorly vented outhouse. It wasn't that it was tucked into a forest so close and dense that leafed branches rubbed the windows. It wasn't any of these things, because any and all of these deficits might have been overcome by a single iota of cheer or vitality. There was just something unspeakably desperate about the place. It was like a three-legged dog, or an aging rock star playing the local dive bar.

"We've got to get out of here," I told Penny late one night, shortly after we'd flopped our exhausted bodies on the mattress tucked beneath the eaves. We'd spent the day framing the floor system of our soon-to-be (but clearly, not soon enough) home, staggering under the weight of brutish two-by-twelve-inch-by-sixteen-foot joists of hemlock. Each weighed approximately as much as a small planet.

It wasn't the first time one of us had expressed that sentiment. It probably wasn't the fiftieth. "I know, I know," she said in a placating tone.

"No, you don't understand!" I was a little panicked, now; I was rising off my pillow, my voice shrill and keening. "We've *got* to get out of here!"

There was something else driving us, too: We simply yearned to be on our land. The yearning was a viral, magnetic force in our bodies and spirits. It could not be resisted, and the only cure was to make the transition as soon as possible, to step through the threshold we now stood upon, to immerse ourselves in the life we had imagined for so long, the one that had kept us awake so many nights, our words barely able to keep pace with our fevered imaginations.

There was a minor problem, which is that we were broke. Every dollar we'd saved had been absorbed by the initial land deal, which had set us back thirty thousand dollars. Half we'd borrowed from a bank; the other half represented the entirety of our life savings, cobbled together one meager eight-dollars-per-hour paycheck at a time. Our shortfall was solved by our friend Jerry, a fast-talking New Yorker who'd cashed in a couple of inherited NYC taxi medallions and was perhaps the only person we knew who possessed both the means and, crucially, the inclination to extend us a loan. Still, the interest rate on Jerry's ten-thousand-dollar loan was 10 percent, which is to say, Jerry might have been a buddy, but he wasn't an altruist.

To raise more cash, we sold our car—a sad little Volkswagen that fetched six hundred dollars—and replaced it with a Dodge pickup of early seventies vintage. The truck was tricolor, the factory green supplemented by swaths of blue and pink. It was ugly, sure, but for two hundred bucks, we sure as heck weren't complaining. There is a certain type of person who sells a six-hundred-dollar car because they are willing to drive something cheaper, and we were that type of person. With Jerry's money, the profit from our vehicle trade, and the help of our friend Rick, a carpenter with biceps so firm and pronounced they might as well have been hewn of wood, we erected the exterior shell of a modest shelter, installing the last of the windows just as the season's first snowstorm rolled up through New England. Rick had gifted us two weeks of his labor as an early wedding present.

To keep expenses low, we'd eschewed a traditional frost wall or basement foundation and instead perched the cabin atop two long rows of concrete piers; each pier was set, eight feet away from its neighbor, into a four-foot-deep hole dug by a splinter-handled spade. By the time all the holes were dug, our palms were pocked moonscapes of blisters. Some nascent and rising, some ripe and juicy, still others turning to hard knobs of callus. I suspect that some of the calluses I have on my hands now were initiated during that digging.

Owing to the slope of the ground, the rearward piers stuck four feet out of the soil, exactly double the recommended maximum height of above-ground exposure. This may have been the cause of the swaying motion that visited our cabin whenever the wind blew, which, owing to the cabin's exposed location, was approximately always. One way to describe the motion is to say that it was sort of like being in a cradle. Another way to describe the motion is to say that it was sort of like being in a cabin that feels as if it's about to tip over.

We lived in the cabin for three years, gradually improving upon it until it featured running water (both cold and, to our rapt amazement, hot), insulation, and a pair of borrowed solar panels that enabled us to run three lights, a radio, and my laptop, although not all at the same time, and, unless the sun was high and bright, not for more than two consecutive hours. We slept atop a futon mattress laid across the rough-board floor of a loft accessed via an aluminum ladder. After the ladder slipped out from underneath a housesitting friend as he was descending, leaving him clinging to the loft edge by his fingertips until he found the courage to jump, we installed a cleat at its base.

For all these shortcomings and many more, we loved that little cabin. Our wedding invitation, mailed just after we'd moved in but before we'd installed insulation or running water, depicted a drawing of our new home's front gable end, with our tandem bicycle leaning rakishly against it, and from just that simple black-and-white sketch, you could sense a particular *rightness* about the scale and form of the structure, as if it knew its place in the world. As if it knew what it was and what it wasn't and had made peace with this knowledge. In a strange way, I could not help but want to emulate it.

Of course, I recognize my bias in all this. It's hard to avoid caring about a structure you've built with your own hands, a place where you can literally point out the faded bloodstains from where you nicked a finger while shaving the edge of a floorboard with a utility knife. The smallness of our home, accompanied by the limited resources with which it was built, ensured a high level of engagement on our part. There was not a single part of the process that did not in some manner or another bear our mark. This is not because we were terrifically skilled. Sure, we had rudimentary construction experience, gleaned primarily from the hodgepodge of jobsites we'd both worked on, but neither Penny nor I had ever advanced beyond the semi-skilled-laborer stage.

Years later, I see how the building of our home is in many ways analogous to the manner in which we educate Fin and Rye. Neither of us had formal instruction in the craft of homebuilding; rather, we relied on our innate curiosity and capacity to learn on the fly. We knew we'd make mistakes (although maybe we underestimated the sheer number of mistakes), but we understood this to be inevitable and therefore not something that could be avoided. When we reached the limit of our skills and resources, we sought out friends and professionals who could facilitate the process. In short, we granted ourselves the confidence that we could actually do such a thing, and while such confidence may seem misplaced and even indicative of an inflated sense of self-worth, I believe it to be nothing more than the confidence all humans are born with but which slowly erodes as they come to perceive learning as existing in isolation from living.

In 2001, we began construction on an addition that more than doubled the square footage of our living space. Again, we comprised the principal labor force in the process, working under the oversight of yet another builder friend, who moonlighted with us on weekends. This time around, we'd secured a construction loan from a local bank, which enabled us to lift the cabin off its piers, excavate and pour a full basement, and commit the summer, fall, and fledgling weeks of winter to expanding our home. It was a span of time that almost perfectly mirrored the gestation of our first child.

Fin's birth did not slow us down as much as we'd expected. For a week or so, we hunkered down, immersing ourselves in the unalloyed joy and occasional confusion of newfound parenthood. "Is his breathing supposed to sound like that?" "Do you think he's too hot? No? Then he must be too cold, right?" "Has he been sleeping too long?" "Is he sleeping enough?" During this period, we did not leave our land, exiting the house only to refill the firewood box, tend to the laying hens, and sweep accumulated snow off the solar panels. It had been a mostly snowless winter thus far, but there was a shift the morning after Fin was born and suddenly it seemed as if the snow would never stop falling. Every morning, we awoke to a fresh layer of white—three, four, five inches—piled atop the layer that had come the previous night, which in turn rested atop the one that had come the night before that. Somewhere beneath it all lay the grass and soil we wouldn't see for another four months.

We ate whatever meals were brought by friends and family and, after a couple days, again began picking away at the innumerable projects standing between us and a finished home. Even in the face of those first sleep-interrupted nights, our sense of relaxation was immense and all-encompassing, and it occurred to us that this was one of the greatest unanticipated benefits of home birth: There was no need to pack up, to be discharged from the hospital, and to buckle our newborn child into a car seat for the drive home. There was no need, because we were already home.

Fin's arrival heralded an expanded sense of what our place—and our relationship to it—could be. I think this was in part an emotional response to our entry into the world of parenting, and in part a result of ways in which we'd structured our lives even before his birth. A few years prior, I'd transitioned to full-time freelance magazine writing, and with the exception of occasional travel, worked primarily at home, an arrangement that generated a tremendous amount of flexibility regarding how I allocated my time. Until the previous fall, Penny had worked on an organic vegetable farm, where she'd managed the field crew. But we'd always planned to have her transition to being a stay-at-home mother, and now, suddenly, she was. There wasn't one stay-at-home parent in our family; there were two. There was no juggling of schedules, no impending sense of Penny's return to work, no need to fret over how to afford child care, no need to worry if we were leaving our newborn son in capable hands.

I feel compelled to explain how we pulled all this off financially. After all, self-employed freelance writing probably isn't on anyone's short list of best ways to make a quick buck, and the same might well be said of vegetable farming. Really, one wonders what occupations we might have chosen that would have been *less* financially remunerative. Competitive finger painting, perhaps? The whole production—buying land, building a house, working at home, choosing to have Penny stay at home—smelled vaguely of a trust fund or perhaps even something criminally nefarious.

Alas, there was no trust fund, nor were we cultivating Vermont's largest grossing cash crop (which is marijuana, if you're wondering). Instead, we had the benefit of skilled and generous friends, as well as a capacity to voluntarily endure more discomfort, if not outright hardship, than has become customary in our nation. Or in any modern first-world country, for that matter. While saving for land, we lived in the turd of a cabin, a tent pitched on land owned by friends, a small A-frame that lacked running water but which did grant us the giddy luxury of electricity, and another funkified rural shack that offered both electricity and running water (opulence, sheer opulence!), with the latter being frequently thwarted by the frigid winter temperatures that turned it to ice. Which is how it would stay until I took up a hair dryer and stuffed myself into the damnable crawlspace where the water lines had unadvisedly been installed.

Once on our land, we again lived without running water or electricity for nearly a year before finally rigging up a rudimentary solar power system. To bring water to the house, we used a generator to run the water pump until the pressure tank was full, at which point we doled out the tap water one precious drop at a time. We bathed in streams and ponds until the onset of winter rendered this practice too painful to continue, at which point we heated pots of water atop the woodstove, to be upended in the old clawfoot bathtub we'd installed in a drafty corner of the cabin.

Certainly, Penny and I benefited from good timing. Buying land when we did, in an era when land could still be bought relatively cheaply, before speculators and unscrupulous lenders had driven prices skyward, was not a calculated decision. We were merely fortunate to be in the market before the market froze us out. Perhaps we still could have managed to purchase our land ten or fifteen years later than we did, but there's little doubt that doing so would have required assuming enough debt to have profoundly impacted our lives. It cannot be overstated just how enabling a factor our manageable debt burden has been, simply for having granted us autonomy over our days. This autonomy provides us the freedom necessary to grow our own food, and it similarly enables me to write for a living. It enables Penny to stay home. And it certainly enables us to provide Fin and Rye the freedom to learn as they do.

I am generally loath to dispense unasked-for advice, but on the subject of debt, I feel obligated to speak up, because there is perhaps no easier way to lose control of your life than by borrowing money. This is not to say you should never borrow. This is not to say that debt cannot be liberating. Indeed, for us, it was. It is only to say that debt should be utilized in full awareness of its tremendous power to define practically every aspect of your life.

We made our final mortgage payment in 2008, and now inhabit a home that, imperfections aside, is perfectly ours. Our house is still unfinished, perhaps terminally so, and I have come to understand this "done enough" state as a common curse of the owner-built home. Somehow, our home became bigger than anything we'd imagined, and it is not the draft-free vessel we'd intended. Winter winds sift through all the small mistakes inherent in our learning and thrift: the window I installed slightly out of square, and the gaps between ill-fitting beams; the cheap single-pane glass that separates our living room from the frigid January air.

So be it. This is our home. It is where Penny and I were married, where our sons were conceived, and where they came into the world. To be granted the honor of dying a natural death under the same roof I screwed down over the course of an insufferably hot

August weekend, my tools slippery with the sweat of my exertion, the back of my neck crimson and peeling under the high sun, would be a blessing so precious I almost dare not mention it, as if giving it voice might somehow alter my hoped-for outcome.

If it seems morbid that I consider my death, and more so that I have specific hopes for how and where I might die, I assure you it feels precisely the opposite. Three years ago, my friend Jim, the same friend who helped me raise our windmill, who loaned us our first solar panels, and who assisted with so many projects that to erase his mark on our home would require nothing short of demolition, died in his sleep of massive heart failure exactly two weeks before he and his wife were to adopt newborn twin girls.

The experience of Jim's passing radically altered my understanding of death, in no small part because his family did an unusual and wonderful thing: they left his body in his bed, and for three days opened their doors to anyone who wished to visit. I remember how it was to see him lying there, and how on the drive to the home he shared with his wife, at one point I flicked on my blinker to make a U-turn, certain I could not face the sight of his body.

I felt the same when Jim's father called to ask if I'd help with the burial, help lift him into the coffin, help carry him down the stairs and out the door, help set him in the ground and fill the hole atop him, only fifty feet from where he died, only fifty feet from where, so many years before, I'd helped my friend raise the frame of his house just as he'd helped Penny and me with ours. All I could think about as we shoveled was the weight of all that soil and the permanence of being placed beneath it. How could I do such a thing to someone I loved? But having done that thing, I can no longer imagine how it could have been any other way.

Is it strange that being so close to my friend in death has made me more comfortable with the prospect of my own? I think not, because it has taught me that as hard and as grief-filled an experience as death can be, it can also be a thing of enormous beauty and grace. It is the natural order of things, and as downright unfair as it may seem for a forty-three-year-old man to die two weeks before he was due to adopt his infant children, even that perceived injustice is part of nature's story. My friend's time was shorter than those of us who loved him would have chosen, but that painful fact does not diminish the gift of his friendship. It does not diminish his parting gift to me, the knowledge of how I wish to die, if I am fortunate enough to choose such a thing.

On our bathroom wall, Penny has tacked a poem. I do not read it every day, but I see it every day, and I know it well enough that I no longer need to read it, anyway. I cannot say where she came across it, but I do know it was written by a man named Jeff Bickart in the months before he died of melanoma at the too-early age of forty-eight. Along with the passing of my friend, it tells me something about how I wish to conclude the story of my life on this piece of land. And for that reason, it also tells me something about how I want to live.

The End

There is no where from here for me.
Our children may choose other things,
this land pass into other hands.
I will be here on the hillside,
lying in a shallow grave,
covered by the native stones,
gone to rest in native ground;
mossy rocks, a gentle mound,
bones sweetening the acid soil.

Ask the Cows

Once again we awoke to the sound of rain slapping the metal roof over our heads. There are many things a tin roof is good for—shedding snow, thriftiness and ease of installation, longevity—but none compare to its excellence in transmitting the sound of raindrops upon contact.

The rain has been incessant. Everywhere you go, first-cut hay remains standing. Perhaps not all of it, but plenty enough, growing taller and stemmier and less palatable by the minute. It's a full month past when most farmers prefer to be finished with first-cut, in part because the nutritional content is vastly superior before so much precious plant energy is expended in the seed head, but also because there's a fairly simple rule of haying, which says that you can't take second-cut until you've taken first-cut, and you darn well can't take third until you've taken second. In other words, it's not only that the first cutting will be of reduced quality, it's that there will be less time for second and third cuts to rise from the soil.

We return from chores, soaked at both ends: our heads and shoulders by the rain that is falling, and our feet and lower legs by the rain that has fallen and now clings to the pasture grass that is growing by inches per day. Everything is lush and verdant, almost overwhelmingly alive. Our boots are permanently waterlogged, our feet wrinkled and clammy.

The boys are unfazed by the constant deluge. Indeed, they seem to hardly notice it, and not for the first time I wonder to what extent our children's reactions are learned, rather than innate. Is it possible that the only difference between a child who plays in the rain and one who does not is that the latter has been taught to avoid the rain?

I have little patience for lament regarding forces over which we have no control, and the same could be said of the majority of the famers I know, whose very livelihood is dependent on such forces in ways that mine is not. I do not hear complaints from these men and women; commentary, sure, perhaps a sigh, a roll of the eyes, a shrug of the shoulders. But not complaints. Complaining takes energy; it is a brittle and hollowing force, not unlike anger or judgment. It does nothing to advance the human intellect and spirit, and therefore it is best saved for moments that are truly worth inflicting these wounds upon ourselves.

All this rain has reminded us how fortunate we are to inhabit a piece of land that drains well. Despite the sodden state of things, the gardens are (mostly) looking hale and hearty, and the critters are their usual implacable selves; I've long thought that cows might be a better model for human behavior than the majority of our so-called leaders. They are accepting of whatever is offered them, and their default mood seems to be one of quiet contentment. Nip the grass, chew the cud, rest the bones, and all the while the generosity of milk, meat, and manure. Cows don't start wars, or discriminate against cows of different color or predilections. Cows don't aspire to create legacies, or to leave any evidence of their passing beyond clipped tufts of grass and steaming piles of manure.

Soon enough, it'll stop raining. Soon enough, I suspect, everyone'll be talking about how dry it is, about how we sure could use a day or two of rain or we're not even going to get a third cut of hay at all. And the cows? They'll be gathered under the same fence-line maples they gathered under back when it wouldn't stop raining, still nipping the grass, still chewing the cud, still resting the bones. Because that's the great thing about trees: rain, sun, snow, whatever—they'll shelter you no matter what.

7

The Downside of
Convenience

IN THE EARLY YEARS of Fin's and Rye's unschooling, Penny and I struggled to determine to what extent organized, away-from-home activities should fit into their learning. This struggle originated at least in part from our own childhood experiences. Penny in particular had been immersed in team sports from an early age. She was a player of such devotion that she often played on two sports teams concurrently, even while recovering from one of the multiple knee surgeries she underwent. Of course, this meant that the majority of her hours not dedicated to school were instead given to field, court, and physical therapy.

Since I was overweight and generally disinclined to demonstrate my lack of skill and agility any more than absolutely necessary, team sports did not play much of a role in my childhood. I have a vague memory of playing on my grade school's basketball team, and I recall that on a few occasions, when our team was already so far ahead or behind that nothing I might do on the court could in any meaningful way influence the outcome, I was allowed a few minutes of action. But despite the dearth of my participation in team sports, I saw how the majority of my classmates were in one way or another immersed in the culture of extracurriculars, and I came to understand this as the norm. It wasn't merely sports, of course. There was theater, music, dance, debate club, horseback riding, Scouting, and probably many others I wasn't even aware of.

Naturally, the list has only expanded over the years, and the advent of the Internet has created an entirely new genre of virtual groups and clubs.

Like so many of our choices surrounding the boys' education, this culture was at odds with our innate sense of what felt right for us. As the boys grew to the age when organized activities became an assumed part of their lives, the disparity between the force of this assumption and our desire to avoid becoming swept up in the inevitable busyness these activities required became a source of conflict for us.

"Should we be doing more?" Penny asked me one evening. "Do we need to provide them with other experiences?" The issue had come to a head after Fin expressed an interest in Little League baseball; the boy has always had a knack for accuracy, demonstrated first by his abilities with the bow and arrow and second by his talents with a baseball. He throws straight, hard, and true, stinging my palm with every pitch, and although he's been exposed to few team sports, we pass the local ball field frequently. There, he saw the teams gathered each spring, either in practice or in competition, and his curiosity was evident in the way he pressed his forehead against the window as we rolled by.

In principle, Penny and I had nothing against him joining Little League; one year we even went so far as to pay the seasonal fee, and Fin spent his spare hours pummeling hay bales with a baseball in anticipation. Ultimately, not enough kids in our small town signed up to field a team, for which Penny and I were mildly relieved. We'd written that check with no small amount of trepidation, because we'd witnessed how organized sports and other activities had profoundly disrupted families we knew, many of whom educated their children at home. In fact, it seemed to us as if the homeschooling families we knew were even *busier* than those families whose children attended school, perhaps out of a sense of needing to compensate for the lack of "opportunities" their kids weren't getting in the classroom.

Our quiet observations regarding the impact of extracurricular activities on these families slowly resolved our conflict. It seemed to us that nearly everyone we knew was always running to one event or another, rushing through dinner to get to a practice or lesson, or even eating in the car. Weekends were often devoted to recitals, or games. "How are you doing?" we'd ask when we ran into friends in town. "Oh, busy, busy. It's just crazy," was the common reply.

Fin and Rye were not shut-ins. Already, both took music lessons, Fin attended a weekly daylong wilderness-skills program, and every Monday, Rye spent the morning with his mentor, Erik. But in comparison to the majority of their friends, our sons' schedules were uniquely relaxed. They might as well have been on permanent vacation.

Interestingly, the boys have rarely asked for more activities. Even our close call with Little League was more a result of Penny's and my early uncertainty than a direct request from Fin. The following spring, he inquired after Little League again, but by that point Penny and I were more secure in our sense of what was right for our family. Still, we did not deny him, and instead explained what joining Little League would mean, how it would take time away from all the other things he loved. There would be less time to shoot his bow, to hunt squirrels, and to play with his brother and his friends. To our admittedly great relief, he decided against baseball.

It is no original thinking on my part to suggest that the business of being a child in this country is rapidly disappearing into an abyss that consists not only of programs and tests but also of extracurricular activities. Increasingly, it is disappearing into the pixelated screens of the innumerable digital devices that already dominate the adult world, and are rapidly encroaching on childhood. Even activities that were once considered "play," and that occurred beyond the gaze and attention of adults, where children were free to negotiate the terms among themselves, to work out disagreements and injustices, are being lost to structured and supervised games and competitions. After all, who has time to just "play" anymore?

In his book *Free to Learn*, Peter Gray writes about the demise of true play, and how school—and, I would add, the expectations set by the culture of schooling, to which even homeschoolers frequently submit—has largely expunged self-directed play from our society:

The school-centric model of childhood has taken increasing hold over time and affected all aspects of children's lives. Playgrounds are no longer places where children go and play freely with one another, but are places of coaching and teaching, led by adults. Children are sorted there into age-segregated groups, just as they are in school. In the home many parents today, in implicit acceptance of the school-centric model, define themselves as teachers of their children. They look for "teaching moments," buy educational toys, and "play" and talk with the children in ways designed to impart specific lessons. No wonder parent-child interactions these days are often accompanied by lots of eye rolling and "whatevers" from the children. Home life begins to become as tedious as school.[1]

Indeed, for a time it felt to Penny and me as if we had to actively resist pressure to enroll Fin and Rye in adult-directed activities. Knowing of Fin's physicality and love of movement, friends and family suggested signing him up for martial arts; when they became aware of Rye's penchant for drawing and painting, they suggested art lessons. It wasn't that anyone was particularly forceful in these suggestions; the force we felt compelled to resist was an interior one, the combination of the assumptions set by our own childhoods, along with the observation that everyone else was doing more than we were, and finally, the gentle, well-meaning suggestions that perhaps our boys would enjoy being part of these programs.

Obviously, not all adult-directed, extracurricular activities are detrimental to children. For us, it is not so much that any one of the activities our boys might participate in—be it Little League, wilderness-skills school, banjo lessons, or martial arts—is something to be avoided. Rather, it's the accumulation of these activities to the point where our children have little time for self-directed play and our family is caught up in the bustle of practices and games and recitals and performances. We've flirted with this bustle enough to know it has the power to pull us away from our home and our appreciation of it. We know it has the power to fragment our family, to suck us into the vortex of "busy" and "crazy." We know it is worth resisting.

All of this brings me to the central challenge of our unschooling, which means it also brings me to the central challenge of our parenting. It's not our *only* challenge, but it is the one that on a day-to-day basis reminds Penny and me that we have not chosen an easy path.

Put simply, the freedom to self-determine how to pass so much of their time has cultivated a certain sense of entitlement in my sons. I wrote of this briefly in an earlier section of this book, but the subject deserves further examination, if only because it is the place where the majority of our conflict arises. In short, Fin and Rye are enormously particular about how they pass their time. In the absence of school's daily schedule and demands that they must adhere to it, they have come to believe that their time belongs to them, and they are not always eager to deviate from whatever task they've set their minds upon.

Of course, this sense of entitlement does not absolve them of the daily tasks for which they are responsible. They know full well they are expected to care for their goats, and that certain contributions to the family's well-being are expected. They know that Sunday mornings are when our family splits and stacks firewood, and they know that come winter, they'll be asked to ferry endless armloads of that very wood from shed to stove.

Often, Fin and Rye do what is asked of them willingly, but often they do not, and my anecdotal observations suggest to me that they are uncooperative somewhat more frequently than many of their peers. Some of this, I think, is simply the result of temperament. My sons are fiercely passionate creatures, afflicted by a degree of willfulness that can fray my patience until only a single, slender strand holds it together. In these moments, my patience hanging in the abyss, I find it helpful to remind myself that this did not just happen. Our boys did not just decide to be opinionated and occasionally obstinate. Oh, no. They learned it from us.

The notion that our children's contrariness might be an inherited trait didn't occur to us until one day a few years ago, when Penny was bemoaning the boys' stubborn natures to a friend. "They hardly ever do what I ask," said Penny. "It's like they do whatever they want and think that's the way it should be."

Her friend gave one of those quizzical looks you give someone when you're wondering if it's really possible they don't see the truth dangling right in front of them. "But that's exactly the way you and Ben are," she replied. "You've arranged your lives so you can pretty much do whatever you want, and you think that's the way it should be."

Whether or not Penny's friend thought this was admirable wasn't entirely clear, but her observation prompted us to consider the many choices we've made that have allowed us to live as we wish to live, but have been inconvenient or simply vexing to others. Both of us left school (Penny dropped out of college), abandoning the presumed security of formal education for a self-directed and more financially tenuous path. When we had children, we flat-out forbade our respective parents from gifting the plastic baubles and electronic gadgetry so common to most families. To their immense credit, both Penny's parents and mine have accepted these restrictions with equanimity, but I've no doubt they silently chafe at them. Even now, they know to ask before presenting the boys with gifts, because, as we are forever reminding them, even thoughtful gifts of useful items can create an excess of stuff.

In short, Penny and I are particular about the influences we allow into our lives, and even more so, about how we pass our time. I like to think of it as being discerning, rather than picky, but I suppose there's really not much difference, and my point isn't to examine whether or not this is a laudable quality but instead to better understand the roots of my sons' frequent mulishness. Furthermore, it is important for me to remember that while my sons' projects and pastimes often strike me as frivolous—do they really need another nailed-together scrap-wood implement for whatever convoluted game they've dreamed up?—their work is as important to them as mine is to me. It might seem perfectly reasonable for me to interrupt their game with a request to help with some task or another, but in truth it is little different than having them interrupt my work in the hope that I might assist them with the design of their latest contraption.

This is all compounded by our choice of an educational path that provides them with so much command of their time, and also that we've always encouraged them to question what they are told. As Penny often reminds me when I am seething about my sons' lack of cooperation or general reluctance to take what I tell them at face value, that questioning will inevitably extend to us. Encouraging our sons to think critically is one of most important aspects of their education; it is also the one that foments the most conflict.

There's often a misperception that unschooling parents don't do much. That they just let their kids run willy-nilly while the adults go about their days. That unschooling is, when all is said and done, easy. In this family, at least, nothing could be farther from the truth. In this family, unschooling is not easy, or convenient. It demands significant reservoirs of thought and patience and, as I've pointed out, presence. Many parents aren't all that accustomed to being patient and present for their kids anymore, if only because they're simply not given the opportunity to be patient and present. Jobs get in the way. School gets in the way. After-school activities get in the way. As I have learned—as I am still learning—patience and presence are muscles that must be developed and exercised regularly. Some of us may be born with more or less of these qualities than others, but no one is born with them fully realized. More than once, I have heard some version of this comment from other parents: "I'd love to do what you're doing, but I just couldn't be around my kids that much. We'd kill each other."

I understand the sentiment because I've felt the sentiment. Penny, too. It is not easy or convenient to be parents to children who think critically. It is not easy or convenient to be parents to children who feel a strong sense of ownership over their time. Furthermore, it is not easy or convenient to be parents to children who are encouraged to participate in the day-in, day-out work of running a small farm. We made a conscious decision early in the boys' lives to sacrifice a degree of order and convenience so they might "work" alongside us, and this has required us to relinquish control in ways we could never have imagined.

Some of this relinquishing involved accepting the inevitable mistakes and messes that result from their learning—the row of fledgling beets they pulled, thinking they were "weeds," or the folded-over nails in the cowshed siding from their early hammering efforts—and some of it was simply letting go of our expectations regarding how long a particular task might take. It takes a hell of a lot of patience to include young children in productive work, and it requires humbling yourself to the reality that it is not going to be as "productive" as you'd like. Except of course it is, because some of what you're producing is a child with confidence, skills, and resourcefulness. But you have to take a pretty long view to see those things, and I don't think humans are particularly good at taking long views. At least, not in this day and age.

For us, owing to the unique particulars of our lives, with both of us working at home, lending our presence to Fin and Rye hasn't been nearly as hard as simply letting go. Penny and I have always been doers; put simply, we like getting things done, and incorporating small children into the process of getting things done all but ensures that less will get done. There's just no way around it.

I still get impatient from time to time, but not very often. Part of this is because I have genuinely become more patient over the years. It's a slow and never-finished process, not unlike developing gratitude or generosity. The other part is that the boys have actually evolved into legitimately productive contributors to home and farm. They no longer pull up beets by mistake. They don't bend nails anymore. Or no more than I do, anyway. But to learn how not to bend nails, they had to bend some. To learn how not to pull up beets, they had to pull some.

It has always bothered me to see how some parents chase their children away from productive jobs. I have seen it many times, and while I understand the impulse, I have little empathy for the short-sightedness of it, because the truth is that long before they are capable of truly helping, kids desperately want to contribute.

Like all of us, children just want to be needed. It's our job to make sure they actually are.

THE PRACTICE

We do chores twice each day, 7 days each week, 365 days each year. Where we live, there's nothing unusual about this; many of our neighbors adhere to similar schedules, and have for half a century or more. Sometimes I consider the math: Twice daily multiplied by 365 is 730, multiplied by fifty years is ... 36,500. Thirty-six thousand chore times. It is almost impossible for me to fathom, it feels insurmountable. But of course it is not.

Sometimes, chores are just chores: haul the water, throw the hay, run the fence. Cold, hot, wet, dry. Hurried. But often, I think of chores the way I suspect some people think of a practice—meditation, or yoga, or prayer. Maybe aikido or a musical instrument. I like to think of chores this way; it seems to give me license to sink into them, to inhabit them in a way that would otherwise elude me.

Chores are physical, and frankly don't require great skill, but they're also emotional, intuitive, and, I think, somehow artistic. I find this to be particularly true of chores that involve animals, which so many of ours do. You cannot live with animals and not have a relationship with them, not be affected by them. You cannot live with animals and not come to know something about them as individuals, each with his or her unique quirks of personality, like the way our milk cow Apple always pauses on her morning walk to the barn to twist her head so that she might address a hard-to-reach itch with her tongue. She twists to the right, then to the left, then back to the right, and you have no choice but to stand and wait until she's ready to move again, and while you're waiting, you do what you always do: look out across the valley below, obscured by the mist of a soft rain or basking in the honeyed glow of the rising sun. Stranded by a cow's itch. Sometimes the greatest blessings come disguised as inconveniences.

I get up most days around five or five thirty. I do not set an alarm. In the summer, when it's light or near enough to being light, I head straight outside. In fall and winter, when daylight is still an hour or more away, I start a fire, make a cup of coffee, sit for a while, and let myself adjust to the day while the rest of the family goes about their slow rousing. There is no electricity in the barn, anyway, and while I could wear a headlamp, I prefer to wait until the sky brightens enough to light my path.

If I'm honest, there are mornings I don't much feel like doing chores. There are mornings when I'd prefer to stay by the stove, where I've parked my chair by the open firebox door, reorienting myself whenever the blast of heat becomes too intense. Of course, I do chores anyway and I can truthfully say that I have never been sorry it had to be so. In part, this is due to the sheer physicality of the work, the way it gets the blood moving on a slow morning, sluicing through the veins and arteries and small capillaries like water driven by some invisible pump. Fifty-pound hay bales will do that; five-gallon buckets of water carried up the hill to the cows will do that. There's something honest about greeting the day with sweat, a small offering, and acknowledgment for the simple good fortune of being alive. Often I think the world would be a better place if everyone had the opportunity to make such offerings, but I know that's presumptuous. I know of my bias.

There's another part to it, and I think it's that chores are an assumption of responsibility in a world that can sometimes feel devoid of such a thing. In a sense, chores are homage to the animals and crops under our care, the fulfillment of a silent promise not only to them but also to ourselves. It's a promise not to take anything for granted, and that we won't forget—for this one day, at least—that we are merely a part of something bigger than we can even imagine.

I cannot overstate our desire for Fin and Rye to know a similar sense of being part of something larger than themselves, to understand their dependence on and role within the cycles and rhythms that define the laws of nature. That define our lives. For this reason, we have always included them in the routines and rituals of this little farm, both the day-to-day and the seasonal. When they were infants, we carried them on our daily rounds, trudging through snow with a child on our back to water the cows, or collect the daily cache of eggs. When they learned to walk, we held their hands as they toddled alongside us.

As I have mentioned, it has often strained the boundaries of my patience to facilitate my sons' involvement. I have gritted my teeth through the inevitable fumbling of their early efforts to join us at our work. I have often wanted to push them aside. How much sooner might I return to the warmth of the house if they did not help me with chores? How much faster could I have stacked that wood alone? How much neater would the stacks be? Or I walk past the cowshed and see the rows of bent-over siding nails and remember the day Fin and Rye spent with hammers in hand, three whacks to the wood for every one that landed on the nail itself, and I remember how I wanted to stop them, to step in and take over. "It's OK," said Penny. "It's just a shed." It *is* just a shed.

It is not like this anymore. Now they greet the day with their own responsibilities in full: goats that must be fed and watered and milked, milk that must be strained and jarred and refrigerated. Now they are not merely "helpers" but actual participants in many of the projects that define our days and seasons. Firewood in winter. Planting in spring. Harvesting in fall. Processing pigs, making sausage and bacon. We do not compel them to assist in these things. And sometimes, they don't. But more often than not, they join us, and I think I know why. Because slowly, over months, seasons, and years, they have developed a sense of responsibility and an understanding of how their contributions better this family and farm. Because they have learned that they are useful. And they know how good that feels.

8

Work of the World

MOST WEEKS, Penny and I take the boys on separate outings. This began a few years back, when it became clear that Fin and Rye could benefit by getting some space from each other. The amount of time they spend in each other's company is immense; on most days, they do chores together, eat three meals together, and spend hours roaming our fields and forest together. Sure, they have friends in the community, but because most of those are shared friendships, playdates do not allow for much separation.

The boys' personalities are so strikingly different, there are times it seems impossible that the melding of Penny's and my DNA could produce such disparate beings. How can it be that Fin is so extraverted, so boisterous and talkative, his energy hot and piercing and room filling, while Rye is so prone to long bouts of introspective silence? It's not that Rye is never rambunctious, but his energy is more self-contained, more readily reined-in and quieted. And it's not as if Fin is incapable of sitting still, reading for hours or perched on a rock at the edge of a productive trout stream. Still, when Fin is in motion, things have an alarming tendency to break, seemingly without having been touched.

I am fascinated by the extent to which creating this separation allows the boys to sink into themselves. True, they are enormously comfortable in one another's company, and despite the occasional cruelties they exchange, they love each other with a fierceness of devotion that is capable of bringing tears to my eyes in those instances when they express it overtly. As a rule, they are exceptionally generous with each other, as if each feels honor-bound to abide by some unspoken agreement regarding the sharing of unanticipated gifts or treats. For his ninth birthday, Rye received a number of trout flies from his uncle. The flies were encased in a hinged box, and I could see the quiet look of envy that fell across Fin's face when his brother lifted the lid. Rye saw it, too. "Fin, you can have some," he said, extending his hand. "You can keep yours on this side of the box, and I'll keep mine on the other." And I recall when Fin was given a bar of chocolate from his instructor at the wilderness-skills program he attends. Chocolate is not a commonplace indulgence in this family, and on the rare occasions it is offered, the boys become covetous. But rather than hoard his stash, Fin carried it in his pocket through the day, only unwrapping it at home, where it could be divvied into four equal portions.

Yet, like all humans, particular dynamics have evolved around their relationships. And because their relationship to each other is at once so strong, so constant, and so informed by their divergent personalities, Penny and I feel as if it is our duty to provide them some space to be apart.

When one of the boys and I are alone together, I notice things that are lost to the noise and on-again, off-again unruliness that pervade my sons' day-to-day existence. In Rye, I notice how he's started to smile in an impishly sideways manner, cocking his eyebrows in concert with the left corner of his mouth. I notice that I no longer struggle to understand certain words, that somewhere along the way, the nearly indecipherable manner in which he pronounced his *r*'s for the first few of his speaking years has resolved itself. I notice that his sense of humor, slower to develop than Fin's, has become well honed and on occasion even biting. I am somewhat relieved by this, because like myself, Fin has always tilted toward unrestrained and not-particularly-funny jokes that elicit little more than polite chuckles from those around him.

Fin: "Want to hear a dirty joke?"

Me (with trepidation): "Uh, sure."

Fin: "A white horse fell in the mud."

This is repeated with some frequency, and is always followed by shrieking laughter from at least one of us.

Another of his favorites:

Fin: "God tells three men that if they jump off a cliff, they'll land in whatever they scream as they're jumping. So the first guy jumps and yells, 'Pillow!' And the second guy jumps and yells, 'Lake!' Then the third guy goes to jump and as just as he's about to leap, he trips on a rock and yells, 'CRAP!'"

Fin's jokes do not do justice to his sense of humor, which can border on ribald but is also represented in his enormous capacity for wordplay. He is prone to improvised limericks, which flow effortlessly off his tongue with no rehearsal. One evening when Fin was ten, we sat down to a meal of fried pork chops. Fin glanced at the cut of meat on his plate and then, in a singsong voice, delivered the following:

Fancy ladies in New York
eating pork with a fork
People in the hills of Cabot
eat it too, but they just grab it

He indulged himself in a chuckle at his own verbal dexterity, then with bare hands snatched up his chop and began eating.

The allocation of a morning per week during which Penny and I would pair up with one of the boys and embark on a small adventure has proven enormously popular. The rules of engagement are simple: The boys can choose what they each want to do, so long as it doesn't cost anything and doesn't require much vehicle travel. Generally, we stick around the home place; fishing is a popular option, as are mushroom hunting and the construction of rudimentary catapults from scrap materials on hand. On occasion, one of the boys will want nothing more than to curl up on the couch and be read to, although this option has become decidedly less popular as they've gotten older. Recently, it occurred to me that it would not be terribly long before they are clamoring for driving lessons.

On a fine morning of the type that can lure even the most wizened Vermonters into believing that summer will never end, it was determined that the four us would pair up and strike off. Outside, the grass was heavy with dew, bent and lush from the accumulated weight of condensed moisture; when I walked down the field to move the cows into a fresh paddock, my boots were quickly soaked through, and despite the rising sun, which was already a hot, fierce orb in the sky, I could feel the remnants of the evening's chill in the water wicking through my socks.

Fin had little trouble deciding upon a Mama-time activity. He wanted to go squirrel hunting, as he'd recently made what he deemed a decent squirrel potpie and was keen to replicate his success. So he loaded the .22, and he and Penny set off for the woods to stalk wild rodent. As they walked out the door, Penny gave me one of those looks long-married people give one another, a look that did not require the company of words to make its point: "Next time, *you're* doing the damn squirrel hunting."

Rye, on the other hand, was having difficulty choosing how to spend his Papa time. I dangled all the usual suspects: fishing, romping through the woods, tractor-driving instruction. No, no, and no. As I mentioned, Rye is quieter and more introspective than Fin; he is more stubborn, too. Whereas Fin can generally be cajoled to do our bidding, once Rye sets his heels, there is no way short of physical force that he will capitulate. I knew that I'd made a mistake in providing so many options, that by giving him so many choices, I'd overwhelmed him. And I suspected that his noes were as much a rejection of that sense of being overwhelmed as they were a response to any of the individual options I'd presented.

As is so often the case in parenting, I recognized my error a few seconds too late, and now needed to extricate myself from the hole I'd dug and stumbled into. I knew Rye well enough that I suspected I'd be extricating for a while, and so it was out of something approaching desperation that I suggested we help Melvin load square bales of hay into his barn. I'd seen Melvin baling at nearly nine the evening before, his tractor and wagon little more than shadows in the gathering dark, and I knew the hay would still be sitting in his barnyard, uncovered. This was fine so long as the weather held. But showers were forecast for the afternoon, and if that hay didn't get under cover, it'd be ruined. It's not that Melvin couldn't have put the hay in the barn by himself, but loading square bales is one of those brute-force tasks, like stacking firewood or digging ditches, that begs for extra hands.

To say I was surprised when Rye agreed would be an understatement. But I knew better than to allow my surprise to register, and so it was that we headed out the door, bound for Melvin's. Already, I was second-guessing my suggestion. First of all, at seven thirty A.M. it was already suffocatingly hot and humid, the air a wet, heavy thing that hung about us like a cloak. I knew it would be hotter still in the loft of Melvin's old barn as the sun rose higher in the sky and the motionless air became thick with heat, and that motes of dust and chaff would fill our lungs with every gulping breath. And second, I knew the bales would weigh somewhere in the range of 50 to 60 pounds. Rye weighs somewhere in the range of 50 to 60 pounds. For a moment, I imagined myself moving a 180-pound hay bale. It was not a flattering picture. But we were in motion, and Rye wasn't merely accepting of the idea, he was downright excited. I'd miraculously extricated myself, and I wasn't about to start digging another hole.

"Can I be in the up part?" Rye asked, meaning that he wanted to be on the receiving end of the hay elevator, which would transport the bales from ground level to the barn's third-floor haymow, a vast, cavernous space that could hold ten thousand bales or more. There is something soaring and almost cathedral-like about the haymows of big barns, as if what transpires there is somehow sacred. Perhaps, in a sense, it is.

We puttered a half mile down the hill to find Melvin, which wasn't that hard, considering he was where he is every single morning of every single day of every single week at seven thirty A.M.

Which is to say, he was milking, bent at the side of one of his big Holsteins, one hand affixing the rubber tentacles of the milking machine to her teats, the other reflexively stroking her side. He arose with enviable speed and agility for a man approaching his eighth decade.

"Melvin, we came to unload the wagon," I said. He looked at me, then at Rye, and almost—but not quite—missed a beat. I could see it in his face, a subtle rearranging around the quick shimmer of doubt. But one does not survive a half century of dairy farming by being flappable, and Melvin wasn't about to sacrifice his composure over a seven-year-old willing to throw square bales. Or willing to try, at least.

A few minutes later, we had the wagon positioned at the bottom of the hay elevator, and Rye had scampered up the rickety wooden ladder into the loft. Per my son's request, it was determined that I would load the elevator from the wagon and that Rye would pile bales in the barn. My confidence that he could hold up his end of the task was thin, and I suspected I'd be scrambling into the loft in short order to extricate him from the mounting pile of hay. But there was nothing to be gained by not trying, so Melvin returned to the rows of big Holsteins in the milking parlor, while I gingerly plugged the elevator's power cord into an exposed outlet. It clattered to life.

We quickly settled into a rhythm. I'd reach through the open gate of the wagon, pluck a bale off the pile, and place it on the elevator, which is little more than a revolving row of large metal teeth set into a steel frame. Leaned up against the barn from ground to third-story haymow, the skeletal contraption looked a bit like a ladder, albeit one tilted at a worryingly shallow angle. The upward-churning teeth sank into the soft underbelly of each bale and carried it up, up, up, until it plopped off the high end at Rye's feet, at which point he would grab the bale by its twin loops of twine and muscle it into the growing pile behind him. Since we couldn't hear each other over the elevator's racket, Rye and I communicated by hand signals. He raised his arms and shook his hands in an imploring motion; at first, I assumed he needed a break, but the motions only became more animated, and I realized he was asking me to place the bales closer together so there would be less down time between each one.

Within an hour, we had the majority of the bales unloaded, and Melvin had finished milking. He emerged from the milk house and we all set to moving them from the big pile Rye had made, carrying each bale a hundred or so feet along the length of the loft floor, to where we could stack them neatly along the back gable wall. Melvin and Rye stacked the low rows and, being the tallest of the bunch, I set the upper layers. Sweat ran thick down our faces, but the work was not unpleasant, and the mounting stack defined our progress in a way that was quietly satisfying, each bale filling a space that, only moments before, had been nothing but air.

In the vast, open space of the barn the pile of hay looked inconsequential, and I knew it was maybe three days' worth of feed for Melvin's small herd of cows—three days out of the two hundred or so days they'd need to be fed hay over the year. And for a moment my mind lingered on all of the essential work that happens that most of us never see, work that goes unheralded and unnoticed, simply so we can pour milk over our cereal or splash cream in our coffee.

The three of us stood for a moment in the broad opening to the haymow, and for a second, I wished I could see us from below with our silhouettes visible against the barn's great, yawing mouth. I thought about how I wish to instill in my boys a quiet appreciation for precisely the sort of work we'd just done and for the people who devote their lives to it. Such work and people are rare, I think, and getting rarer, in this era of mechanization and industry and careers built on little more than the flow of money and information.

How satisfying it was to see those bales stacked in Melvin's listing barn, a wealth that few would understand and none would see but for Melvin, my son, and me. And, I suppose, the cows. I wanted to somehow express this satisfaction to Rye, so that perhaps he might be understand the dignity that comes of honest labor, and that so much of the essential work unfolds in quiet anonymity, receiving neither acknowledgment nor acclaim. But I wasn't sure how exactly to get my point across, and besides, I've long ago learned that my children understand far more than I give them credit for, and it's best to just keep my mouth shut.

I know that our neighbor's life is not always easy. We have been Melvin's neighbor for more than fifteen years, and for more than fifteen years, we have watched him work. And work. I know roughly what he has: a piece of land upon which he is entirely dependent for his livelihood, along with a drafty old farmhouse that requires a dozen cords of firewood each year just to keep the windows from icing over. A barn, in poor enough repair to be as much a liability as an asset. Just enough cows to produce just enough milk to make payments on the equipment to make hay and spread manure. For this, and not much more, he works a dozen hours per day, seven days per week, fifty-two weeks per year, and at sixty-six years of age, the end is not yet in sight, in part because he does not want the end to be in sight, but also because he cannot afford for the end to be in sight. Melvin will work as long as he can possibly work, until the very day and perhaps even minute his body will no longer allow it. It will be enough. It will have to be.

As grinding as this may sound, I have never heard Melvin express anything but gratitude for the life he has chosen. After nearly two decades of seeing him nearly every day, after countless hours of standing in his barnyard talking weather and politics and cows and all the other minutiae that comprise our lives on the hill we both call home, I have never, not once, heard him express bitterness that he does not have more, or that his future looks pretty much the same as his past, that his list of undone tasks form a line stretching farther than his day can accommodate. Perhaps even farther than his life can accommodate.

"I've followed my dream," he told me once. We were standing in his barn at milking time, enveloped in the sweet smell of fermented hay and manure, his cows shuffling to and fro in their stanchions, waiting for their turn with the milking machine. "I've gotten to do exactly what I wanted to do," and as he told me this, I thought about how every winter I see Melvin crossing his pasture in his tractor, driving through the deep snow on his way to the woods, where he'll cut enough firewood to fill the machine's loader. It will last for a day or maybe two, and then I'll see him on his way to the woods again. He always waves broadly when he sees me. He is always smiling. I know that back at his house, the fire has gone cold, or is slowly burning through the final lengths of wood from the previous day's gather. And I thought about how frequently he comments on something he's observed on one of his trips to gather wood; the tracks of an animal, perhaps, or the way you can sometimes see a storm blowing in, the way the sky first crinkles then darkens as weather moves across it.

In my life, I have observed time and again how the people who've taught me the most never actually relayed much information. Oh, sure, I've learned my share of tips and tricks from Melvin, mostly relating to the handling of large animals or other farm-related tasks. But the more important lesson is the one I absorb every time he smiles and waves on his way to collect just enough firewood that his house won't freeze for at least another day. The more important lesson is him standing in his barn in the eleventh hour of a twelve-hour workday, leaning wearily on the hoe he uses to scrape shit into the gutter, telling me he's gotten to do exactly what he wanted to do.

Rye and I left Melvin's covered in drying perspiration and hay chaff. Melvin thanked us, and I knew he meant it, because it is not Melvin's style to express hollow gratitude. I asked Rye if it had been hard for him to move the bales and if he was tired. But he just looked at me out of the corner of his eye, gave me the sideways grin I am coming to love so much, and shrugged.

That night, after chores and dinner and reading, Rye showed me his hands, and the blisters that had already burst. Flaps of skin hung ragged from his small palms. They looked like little flags.

"That was fun," he said, and for a second I thought of asking for clarification. Was it truly "fun," or was it satisfying? Because perhaps this would be a fine opportunity to expound on the difference between the two.

Fortunately, I caught myself just before launching into a teaching moment, and instead merely nodded my head. "It sure was."

At that, Rye rolled over, tucked his ruined hands under his head, and went to sleep.

Letting Them Be

The boys are building a shelter down in the woods, inspired by a recent trip to help raise a barn. The fellows raising the barn—two mid-twenties college buddies who soured on corporate life and went in on a thirty-acre parcel half a stone's throw from the Canadian border—are living for the summer in a netted tent constructed of small trees and a few sheets of metal roofing. The tent is situated on a jut of land by the banks of a stream, and it's impossible not to imagine how it might be to fall asleep there, with the water rushing by and the breeze stealing through the net. I could see my sons' imaginations kick into overdrive the moment they saw the structure; I could tell simply from how their faces were arranged that they'd decided to build one for themselves. This decision had been reached in approximately four-and-a-half seconds. Not a word had been spoken.

The very next morning before Blood had halted his crowing, before the sun was yet full in the sky, before Penny and I had finished morning chores, the boys were down in the woods, scouting locations for their shelter. They'd brought a post hole digger, a handsaw, and numerous sections of baling twine, with which they'd lash the framing posts together.

We called them for breakfast, and they arrived with dirt and bark clinging to their skin. "We've got most of the posts cut," Fin said. "And the holes dug!" Rye chimed in. They ate hurriedly, in a slurping fashion, and then retreated back to the woods.

Three hours later, Rye slipped into the house, left hand tucked into right armpit. "What's going on?" I asked, although by the way he carried himself and how quiet he was, I knew perfectly well what was going on: he'd hurt himself. "Cut myself," he said softly, pawing through the first-aid drawer with his uninjured fingers. He extracted a bandage and the bottle of tree tea oil, and commenced to doctor his wounded digit. I continued washing dishes and tried not to watch out of the corner of my eye.

Two hours after that, Fin tromped through the kitchen and also beelined for the first-aid drawer. "What's going on?" I asked, although again I knew perfectly well: he'd hurt himself, smashed a thumb with his hammer, and blood was oozing out from beneath his thumbnail. "Hit my thumb with the hammer, YOWZA," he said, hopping up and down a little, in an attempt to distract himself from the pain. He pawed through the first-aid drawer with his uninjured fingers, extracted a bandage and the bottle of tea tree oil, and commenced to doctor his wounded digit. I continued preparing lunch and tried not to watch out of the corner of my eye.

By dinner, with no further bloodshed, the boys had erected a sturdy frame. At each juncture of wood, twine had been wrapped and tied. The roof was peaked, and a sturdy ridgepole supported rafters of small red-maple and fir poles. They'd dug a pit off to one side and lined it with rocks to contain their cooking fires. During all of this, they'd asked for and received no help from Penny or me, although clearly one of us would need to cut the metal roofing for them. But otherwise, this project was theirs. The mistakes were theirs. The arguments over how to space the roof strapping were theirs. The small triumph of seeing it assembled was theirs. Even the associated injuries and treatment of them were theirs.

It's taken me a long time, probably longer than it should have, but I think I might finally be learning to let go. To let my boys saw and hammer. To let them negotiate and argue and yell. To let them screw up and start over and screw up again. To let them bleed and to let them stop their bleeding. To let them follow the spark of an idea and see where it takes them.

What do my children most need from me? The answer is humbling: They need me to let them be.

9

Risk and Responsibility

ABOUT SIX YEARS AGO, the four of us began haying with another neighbor. Martha runs a small dairy farm with her sister, Lynn, on the ridgetop across the valley from our holding in Cabot, Vermont. She is sixty-six, sports an unruly mop of jet black hair, and inhabits a body that seems to have been purpose-built for labor. When I see her arms emerging from the rolled-up sleeves of the flannel shirts she wears, even in July, they are all protruding vein and muscle, and I am reminded of those migrating birds that can fly hundreds of miles without food or sleep. Martha even eats like a bird, existing on a sporadic ingestion of calories, along with less sporadic doses of caffeine and nicotine. When we hay, she often forgets about food, and I have learned to put a sandwich into her hands, to say, "Here, Martha, eat this," even if all she's asked for is coffee or a Coke. Paradoxically, she was once an Olympic Nordic skier, and it occurs to me that the same genetics responsible for her athletic prowess also enable her to thrive on this substandard diet.

Our haying arrangement with our neighbor evolved out of mutual needs, in the manner of many rural working arrangements made across generations that came long before mine. In short, what Martha needed was muscle, enough to meet the demands of pulling a few thousand fifty-pound bales from the long metal chute of her baler before tossing them toward the rear of the wagon to whoever is stacking them neatly in a crosshatched pattern for utmost stability. The stability is important, as her hayfield features numerous undulations, like oceanic swells caught at the height of their unfurling. I ride the wagon with my feet spread wide and planted, feeling it pitch and heave beneath me, like some landlocked hillbilly version of surfing. The fact that the brakes on Martha's old John Deere are barely operational dials up the excitement a notch or two, but still I stick the toes of my boots over the edge to hang ten. Then the wagon bucks and it feels suddenly as if I might be tossed under the wheels, and I retreat.

What we needed was simpler: hay for our menagerie of ruminant animals, which generally includes a half-dozen cows, an equivalent count of sheep, and the boys' goats. So a deal was struck, although truthfully, there never was a deal per se. Rather, things sort of took on a life of their own, following a path of crude logic. We'd help Martha and Lynn fill their barn, and once that was full and their livestock were guaranteed another winter of sustenance, we'd fill ours. We'd kick in something for fuel and maintenance, but the bulk of our debt would be paid in sweat and the slightly nauseous feeling one gets at the end of a long day tossing square bales.

Rye was barely more than a toddler when we began haying with Martha; on each wagonload, we'd stack a few bales into a small cubby for him and his brother, and they'd sit there for hours as we traversed the field, the baler sweeping up the windrows of loose hay and pressing them into tight, tied bundles, one of those mechanical sleights-of-hand that has never failed to amaze me.

Over the years, the boys' responsibilities in the hayfield have evolved in concert with their physical abilities and their capacity for sound judgment and reason. When they became strong enough, they were pleased to demonstrate their newfound strength by unloading and stacking the bales; when they became suitably cognizant of their surroundings, attuned to the potential hazards inherent in large machinery, they were allowed to hitch and unhitch the wagons. Last year, they learned to drive the old Farmall tractors we use to pull the loaded wagons back to the barn. Penny and I rode with the hay behind them as the boys idled across the freshly shorn field.

Riding that wagon last summer, my eight-year-old son sitting tall in the seat of the tractor, I found myself remembering the boys' first knives. I'm not sure why; maybe there was something in my sons' careful posture on the tractor that reminded me of how they'd sat with those knives, as if the responsibility actually filled their physical beings, made them more aware of how they carried themselves and how the world perceived them. Perhaps even how they perceived the world.

The boys got their first knives when they were four. This wasn't because four is a magic age at which a child should be outfitted with a wedge of honed steel; in our family, responsibility doesn't have birthdays. Instead, the boys' early exposure to knives was simply an extension of the critical role cutting implements play in our lives. From birth, Fin and Rye saw Penny and me using knives on a daily basis: Slicing through twine on bales of hay, carving spoons, grafting an apple tree. Around here, a pocket or belt knife is not a novelty or an accessory. It's a necessity.

We started the boys on pocket knives with locking blades, with the understanding they were to be used only in our presence. This seemed prudent, given the blade's indifference to flesh and tendon, and also given our older sons' aversion to tranquility. Could Fin really still his restless body enough to use one safely? Frankly, Penny and I were not certain. We kept a pack of bandages close at hand.

We needn't have worried. There was something in the seriousness of the blade and the responsibility granted that transformed our son. Fin would sit quietly for long periods of time, whittling the same stick until it had been reduced to a pile of shavings. He didn't so much seek to make things as to unmake them, to transform whatever slender branch he held into wisps of wood fiber and the experience of that transformation. With every pass of the blade, with every curl of whittled wood, he learned a fraction more about pressure and angle and process.

I know from the reaction we got from other parents that the notion of a four-year-olds' tender palm wrapped around the handle of a pocket knife was unsettling; many would probably feel the same about an eight-year-old at the controls of a tractor. We showed the boys how to safely manage these new tools; it's not as though we handed them knives and left them to tinker and fend for themselves. Still, it wasn't long before Fin and Rye were granted autonomy over the use and care of their tools. Did they cut themselves? Indeed they did, though never very deeply—never as deeply as I, as an adult, have cut myself in only the past handful of months. We put a first aid kit in an easy-to-access kitchen drawer and showed them how to clean and doctor their small wounds.

How protective should we be of our children? And I don't mean just Penny and me, but all parents. It often seems that parents are at once too protective and not protective enough, that having been socialized to accept certain risks but not others, we shortchange our children's sense of responsibility and confidence by "protecting" them from the tools and activities that build these very qualities. Of course, that shortchanging is itself dangerous, and even more so because the danger is abstract. It does not result in blood or tears or broken bones, and therefore, it is easy to pretend it does not exist. And in pretending it does not exist, we allow it to fester.

In her groundbreaking book *The Continuum Concept,* Jean Liedloff recounts her observations while living with the Yequana, an indigenous South American Indian tribe. At first, Liedloff was shocked by the level of so-called danger the tribe's children were exposed to, including machetes and knives, open cooking fires, and swiftly running rivers. Surely, these hazards meant frequent injury and maybe even worse among the tribe's children. But after two-and-half-years of living with the Yequana, Liedloff observed almost exactly the opposite: Despite almost immersive exposure to risks that would make most American parents go cold with fear, accidents and injuries were exceedingly rare.

The operative factor seems to be placement of responsibility. The machinery for looking after themselves, in most Western children, is in only partial use, a great deal of the burden having been assumed by adult caretakers. . . . The result is diminished efficiency because no one can be as constantly or as thoroughly alert to anyone's circumstances as he is to his own. It is another instance of trying to better nature; another example of mistrust of faculties not intellectually controlled, and usurpation of their functions by the intellect, which does not have the capacity to take all the relevant information into consideration.[1]

What Liedloff observed is perfectly logical. When you take responsibility from a child, he becomes less responsible. And as he becomes less responsible, he is granted less and less responsibility. The intellectual rationale for this is again perfectly logical: If a knife is sharp and can hurt a child, we should protect the child from that potential harm. If a tractor is big and ponderous and imbued with the possibility, however small, of an accident, we should protect the child from that possibility.

But what if, as Liedloff contends, the child already has protective mechanisms beyond what our intellect can fathom? Furthermore, what if the opportunity for a child to feel useful is worth the risk of parted flesh? Because to feel useful is a powerful thing. To feel trusted is a powerful thing, and I wonder if that is what I see in my sons' young bodies when they take to the seat of Martha's tractor. I wonder if it's what I remember in the early days of their knife handling, the way it quieted and focused them, the way they appeared just the smallest amount more substantial with those blades unfolded.

Haying with our friends has become a ritual for my family. It is, like sugaring or cutting firewood, a task connected to a particular season, place, and process, work that we have come to know so intimately that we can hardly imagine what our lives were like before it was part of them.

I think about this in the context of Fin and Rye, who have been involved in these rituals almost literally since they were born. Or maybe *ritual* is too strong a word; perhaps it is merely habit born of simple necessity: We make hay because if we don't, our animals go hungry. We cut firewood because if we don't, we are cold.

But no matter what you call it, our boys have known these things since they were infants, and I wonder how these tasks will inform their lives. Of how they have already informed their lives. I recall the look on Rye's face when he learned to drive the tractor, how it shifted from nervous to determined, visible in the slightest subtleties of arranged features and held tension that only a parent could identify. And the huge smile when he finally mastered the clutch and the Farmall lurched into motion, my boy riding it across the field, the smell of drying hay in our noses. Or my sense of Fin, finally allowed to do what he feels like he's been capable of for so long, and how he receives that trust and stores it somewhere inside of him for future reference. It is impossible to say when or how that reservoir of trust will serve him. But I am certain it will.

Or the ties we've formed with Martha and Lynn and Lynn's husband, Roman. They are not ties of mere convenience. Rather, we are bound by mutual need, and I think about how rare this dependence has become. I think about how a couple of haying seasons ago Martha became discouraged—there were breakdowns of equipment and rain and other complicating factors—and she commented to Penny at how ridiculous the whole operation seemed when all around us farmers were putting up hay with modern equipment at a pace that might have been ten times ours. "You are right, Martha," Penny told her. "They do put up more hay. But they are sitting alone in the cabs of their tractors when they do it." Martha's eyes lit up and the tension drained from her face.

Someday, of course, there will be no more haying with our friends. It is an inevitability as certain as Melvin's retirement, as our son's growing older, as the coming of winter at the knife's edge of fall. It is as certain as death. But for now, I have the luxury of knowing that what I contribute on that hayfield and in that barn matters. That hay does not just happen, but must in some way be called forward, given little pieces of myself—sweat, a tired back, the crosshatched welts dried hay leaves on the pale underbellies of my forearms—in exchange for its gift of sustenance.

I suspect this is at the core of what I love so much about haying. It feels like such an honest, tangible exchange. It is so unpretentiously elegant in its simplicity, and there are moments when I'm riding the wagon across the hayfield, or grunting bales into the barn, or just sitting in the grass, letting the breeze dry my sweat to salty streaks, when I feel as if I am in some crude way rubbing against that elegance.

"Pay attention, guys, because you're going to be in charge of this operation before long," Martha tells Fin and Rye when we stop to put a new roll of twine in the baler. She means it, although frankly, the boys seem a little skeptical. And who can blame them? The intricacy of the baler, with its gears, knotters, and web of twine, all of which require frequent intervention. And the sheer mass of the Deere, its rear tires towering high above the boys' heads, its exhaust snorting the rich black smoke of uncombusted diesel. My children have not yet arrived at the conquering age, when the default assumption is that such things can be bent to their will. But they are only human; they'll get there, and Martha knows it. She knows, too, of her own mortality, that even a creature that can fly hundreds of miles without food will eventually grow weary. She jokes that someday we'll have to strap her rocking chair onto the wagon. We'll stick a lit Camel in one hand and a megaphone in the other, and she can bellow orders as we make long, looping passes through the field. The real joke, of course, is that she's not joking.

Not many farmers put up large quantities of square bales these days. Speaking strictly in terms of haying technology, square bales are nearly two generations past their prime. The onset of the square bale's decline can even be traced to a specific year: 1965, which is when the delightfully named Virgil Haverdink was casting about for a master's thesis project at Iowa State University. After a winter of tinkering in the school's machine shop, Haverdink had fabricated a loutish-looking contraption known as the world's first large round baler.

Haverdink cleverly designed the implement so that the finished bales—each of which contained roughly the equivalent of fifteen square bales—would shed water. And because air could not penetrate into the compacted mass of hay, any moisture encapsulated within it would introduce fermentation, rather than mold. The former is entirely palatable to ruminants; the latter can be deadly. This meant that farmers could bale before the forage was entirely dry, which in turn meant they needn't wait for a three-day window of sun to make hay. Indeed, many farmers now put up what is known as "hay in a day."

The modern round bale, then, confers numerous advantages. It turns the phrase "make hay when the sun shines" into a platitude rather than a truism, and by doing so, it extends a callused middle finger to the vagaries of weather. And because the bales are too big to be handled by hand (depending on moisture content, a round bale can weigh upward of twelve hundred pounds), they must be handled by machine. Because they must be handled by machine, no more physical effort is required than that which is necessary to operate the tractor's controls. The upshot? With round bales, an entire winter's worth of hay for an entire farm can be put into round bales by one person, who needn't even touch a single stem of grass in the process.

All of which is to say, putting hay into rounds is quicker, easier, and exponentially more forgiving than putting it into squares. Heck, if you wrap them in plastic, as is common practice in the Northeast, they don't even require shelter. It's not hard to understand why the technology gained widespread adoption in very short order and why you can't drive through Vermont's farmland in the early years of the twenty-first century without passing row upon row of the big white marshmallows of hay.

So I concede the round bale makes a certain kind of logical sense. And in full fairness to Haverdink and the technology as a whole, I should note that we feed a few to our cows every winter. It's enormously convenient to simply fire up the tractor, plop the bale in the paddock, and leave the cows to their ruminating. But doing so always leaves me feeling a little hollow and confused, like I've just gotten something for nothing, and I'm not quite sure if I should be grateful for all the work I didn't have to do, or cheated because I didn't have to do it.

In recent years, I have come to understand that certain moments shape my life by a measure not consistent with their brevity and immediate imprint. These are not the big events, the births and deaths, the unions and separations, which for all their significance are the commonplace joys and tragedies of humanity. Rather, they are splashes in the pool of my existence, small stones tossed into the eddy of my life, like when I glance up at Martha perched on that big green tractor like a sprite riding the back of some great beast, a hundred pounds soaking wet atop twelve thousand pounds of machine, towing another ten thousand pounds or more of hay and baler and wagon, and I marvel at what it means to be human, to be of the species that for better or worse has invented all this stuff, this amazing, crazy, magical *stuff*. I mean, my God, to be towed through a field at the ass end of a twenty-thousand-something-pound chain of steel and rubber and grass? And to have the master of that chain be a cigarette-smoking Olympian with the bones of a bird and the work ethic of an entire anthill? It's almost as if I can feel the small stone dropping through my surface. It's almost as if I am not just the pool but also the shore and I can see those waves rushing toward me.

The field we hay with Martha is at a high elevation, with 270-degree views of everything that makes Vermont the place non-Vermonters wished they lived in, if only it weren't for the blackflies, mud season and, depending on their political leanings, Bernie Sanders. During the rare moments when bales aren't popping out of the chute, I like to look out across those views and remind myself to stop taking so damn much of my life for granted. This works for a day, maybe two, before I retreat back into my old jaded self. But every year, a little more of it sticks, and I remain hopeful that by the time I'm Martha's age, and maybe even sooner, gratitude will have become habitual, an ever-present backdrop from which to greet the world.

I like to sing as I chuck bales, and there's something about the brute physicality of the task that pushes me toward the juvenile, if not downright infantile, favorites of my youth, such as Van Halen's

"Hot for Teacher" or perhaps "Rock You Like a Hurricane" by the Scorpions.

On haying days, Penny mixes thick milk shakes and we drink them on the ride home, the four of us crammed into the cab of our old Chevy. We idle down the gravel road from the hayfield; the loaded wagon pushes us, and I ride the brakes. Oncoming traffic gives us a wide berth, and wisely so. Everyone waves in that two-fingers-off-the-steering-wheel way rural Vermonters wave, as if afraid to commit to even this brief, passing relationship. I can smell the warm hay, the hot brakes, and the chopped-up sprigs of mint Penny puts into the sweet slurry of cream, egg, and maple syrup. I can smell the sweat that has risen, flowed, and is now drying on my skin. It is not sour, or at least, not yet. My teeth hurt from the cold drink, and I know that my day is nowhere near over. There is this wagon to unload, and yet another to fill. There will be more tomorrow.

But for the seven or eight minutes it takes to get home, I am afforded the satisfaction only hard labor can provide, and I think ahead to the coming winter, when I will pull each of these bales out of our barn, one by one, extracts of summer in an iced-over world. And I will remember how it happens every year that I improbably recognize a bale or two—maybe a runt from an early pass, when we were still fiddling with the baler settings, or maybe one from the field's edge, with an identifying stick woven in, shed from the old maples that line the northern fringe, overseers of more hay and toil than I can imagine.

And I'll stand in our snow-packed barnyard for a minute, holding the bale, wrenched back to the moment I hauled it off the chute and passed it to back to Penny or one of the boys as Martha guided the tractor down the long windrow, the smell of grease and diesel and drying hay riding softly on the summer air. It's not a moment frozen in time, but rather just the opposite: A moment so fluid it can travel across weeks and even months to be with me at six o'clock on a January morning, to a point roughly equidistant from the haying season before and the haying season to come.

Then I walk up the short hill to the paddock, release the compressed hay from the confines of its twine, throw it over the fence, and leave the cows to their breakfast.

ONLY HUMAN

The season's first big snow finds me on the new shed roof by seven A.M., trying to nail down the last few sheets of tin before the storm begins in earnest. Already, the air is thick with driven flakes. When I look up from my task, I see the cows, bent to their feed, broad backs coated with white. I see the boys, sleds in hand, trudging through the accumulating snow. They are yelling. Maybe they are arguing, or maybe they are just yelling to notice how the snow hushes their voices. I yell, too, but they don't hear or, if they do, don't acknowledge hearing. They are getting older, learning that I can be ignored.

It is 16 degrees Fahrenheit. The bare fingers of my nail-holding hand burn with the cold, and I have to stop every three or four nails to tuck the fingers into my armpit. Beneath my feet, the tin is extraordinarily slippery, and twice I almost slide over the roof's edge. It is not a long drop, so I allow myself to enjoy the sensation of sliding, knowing that even if the worst should come to pass, it wouldn't be that bad. But I stop in time.

I have always loved winter. For years, it was for the skiing, the cut-loose feeling of falling down a mountain, of being at once in control and out of it, crossing over that invisible line so often and so frequently, I rarely knew which side I was on. I still covet this sensation, but have noticed a shift in my appreciation of the season. Maybe it is age. Maybe it is fatherhood. Or maybe it just is. Whatever the reason, I find it in the sight of those cows, uncomplaining as the snow piles atop their hides. They stand so still, as if giving the storm permission to fall upon them.

Once, I a saw a branch break under the weight of accumulated snow. I heard the crack, and a moment later the sudden whump of it landing on the ground, and I could not help thinking about the single flake that proved to be one flake more than the branch could hold. It was like an old man's final breath. One breath too many. If only he'd stopped breathing earlier perhaps it could have been avoided.

Even the absurdity of laying roof on a 16-degree morning, in a snowstorm, no sure footing to be found. I should be cold—hell, I am cold—should be miserable, should probably wait for the storm to pass. It's not my work ethic that keeps me up here, nor some misguided notion of what defines valor. Believe me, I have no surfeit of these particular traits, although it is true that a small part of myself will measure its worth against the portion of the job that remains unfinished at day's end. It is true that I can feel myself taking strength from the sight of those cows, from the sound of the boys whooping in the cold.

But it is also true that the settled, elemental nature of winter soothes and fortifies me in a way I can't quite define. I do not see it as a battle with the elements; it is more like an acquiescing to them, a simple, humble acknowledgment that there is so much beyond my control. The cows know it; perhaps I have learned some of it from them. I'm pretty sure the boys know it, too, though it probably won't be long before they forget. They are only human, after all.

10

The List

On a late October morning, a full sixteen years after Penny and I first walked our land, Fin and Rye rose before first light. They dressed quickly, pulling frayed sweaters over holey long johns, stepping into pants stiffened by the accumulated essences of their wandering. Sleep-tousled hair was tucked into woolen hats, rubber boots fitted to growing feet, leather gloves slid over the soft hands of youth.

Penny and I watched from the kitchen window as they waddled down the field under the weight of their provisioned pack baskets, their progress marked by the bobbing, darting beams of their headlamps. The baskets the boys wore were themselves products of their own hands, loaded with axes and traps and lure. Wire and water. Behind us, the woodstove creaked and ticked, the small sounds of metal expanding with the rising heat, the particular, acrid odor of warming iron and wood smoke.

The previous day, the opening day of trapping season, Fin and Rye had spent nearly a dozen hours setting traps across our land and Melvin's. They'd set traps for muskrats and mink, raccoon and fox. They'd set traps on the banks of a stream, and at the bases of fence posts, or tucked into the cleft made by a junction of tree roots. They returned just as the last tendrils of daylight were being lost to the thick, clouded darkness of night. They ate and collapsed into bed, falling into the arms of their unconscious and whatever stories it held for them.

That Fin and Rye would become trappers had never crossed our minds. It was almost inconceivable, like imagining they would take an interest in hairstyling or opening a fast-food franchise. Penny and I did not trap, nor did we so much as know anyone who trapped. To us, trapping seemed both crude and cruel, and our interest in fur as anything more than the outermost layer of an animal was nonexistent. Sure, we raised animals for slaughter and consumption, but this felt like something different. The deaths of the creatures under our care were immediate and painless, and the very purpose of their living was understood from the day of their conception.

"What do we do?" Penny asked, when it became apparent that our sons' interest in trapping would not pass of its own accord. It had been two years since it had blossomed, and rather than wane, their fascination had only intensified. We had told them of our concerns. We talked of cruelty and of dresser drawers packed with clothing made of cotton and wool; we did not need the fur or the flesh these animals would die to provide. The boys didn't need whatever money might be gleaned by selling the furs, money that trickled down through a series of exchanges that depended on someone, somewhere wanting to wear the coat of a wild creature for no other purpose than to fulfill a manufactured emotional desire. We had told them of all this, and on more than one occasion, we had outright said no.

But even in the face of our refusal to facilitate their desire to trap, Fin and Rye persisted. They immersed themselves in books on tools and technique, and practiced assembling the primitive traps they'd read about. They set deadfalls for mice, and figure fours for rabbits. All the while, they tried to educate us about the realities of trapping. "It's not like the old days, when the traps had teeth," Fin told us repeatedly. He showed us pictures of modern traps, with offset, laminated jaws that held without wounding, and the quick-killing conibear traps that delivered instant death.

Still, for three full years we refused. And for three full years, our sons continued building traps, along with other hunting devices: bows and arrows, throwing sticks, and an elegant Native American spear-throwing device known as an atlatl. The ingenuity and sheer effort invested in their weapons was becoming increasingly difficult to ignore.

It wasn't until Fin was six that any of these devices bore fruit; his first kill was a chipmunk, which he shot off the branch of a maple tree with a homemade bow and arrow. Penny and I had never needed to explain that we would not tolerate killing for sport; our sons had always understood that any animal they took would be utilized to the greatest extent possible. Now that he had a dead rodent in hand, I half expected my son to change his tune. But he cheerfully went about dressing and skinning the small creature, and as I watched him, I could see that he'd prepared for this moment a thousand or more times in his head. Each movement, each slice and swivel of the blade was true, and within minutes he'd stretched and tacked the soft, tawny skin to a scrap of lumber for drying. He laid a fire in the fire pit and impaled the small carcass on a skewer, and soon the odor of roasting chipmunk wafted through the air.

"Here, Papa, try some," implored Fin when he deemed it suitably blackened. He extended a scrap of stringy meat in his greasy fingers. His lips were lustrous with chipmunk fat, and I tried not to recoil. It was my son's first kill, after all. The least I could do was take a bite. I held the blessedly small bit of meat in my palm, before popping it into my mouth in a single, swift motion, like one takes a bitter pill. I chewed tentatively, unleashing an indeterminate meaty flavor. It was not delicious, but neither was it disgusting. It was just . . . meat. I chewed once or twice more and swallowed, relieved to have fulfilled my fatherly duty without vomiting. Following Penny's obligatory sample, the remainder of the chipmunk was shared between Fin and Rye, and they gnawed the flesh off the bones as enthusiastically as if they were dining on joints of prime beef.

Clearly, the boys were serious, and after that chipmunk made its journey down their alimentary canals, Penny and I could no longer deny just how serious they were. And we began to understand why trapping held such appeal. The boys desperately wanted to hunt, not merely for sport but to provide their own meat and hides. Fin's first kill aside, bow hunting is incredibly hard. Further successes would be few and far between. They weren't ready for firearms, or perhaps Penny and I weren't ready for them to have firearms. But trapping was different. It was accessible, and after witnessing their commitment, it no longer felt right to deny them something they were so passionate about. Furthermore, was our sons' desire to trap really so wrong, or could it be that Penny's and my perceptions of trapping lacked depth? Because what, really, had informed those perceptions? Certainly not experience. Certainly not any firsthand knowledge of what it all meant or could mean.

In hindsight, I see now that our boys had done precisely what children will do: they'd surprised us, and in full candor, we struggled for a time with not being disappointed by this surprise. Where had their passion for hunting and trapping come from? Not from Penny and me. Not from their grandparents, or the parents of friends. We knew people who hunted and trapped, but most of these people were on the periphery of our lives. They were not part of our immediate culture, and we were fine with that. From birth, we'd immersed them in nature, expecting this immersion to instill in them our particular idea of reverence for the natural world. It was a version of reverence that did not include bows and bullets and pack baskets loaded with traps.

Yet the boys had always been drawn to the wild and to the inevitable death and consumption of living creatures that is as natural to the wild as Grande Soy Milk Cappuccinos are to the city. Fin and Rye have been fascinated by tales of wilderness adventure since they were old enough to express such preferences. One of their favorite books is *Hatchet,* by Gary Paulsen. *Hatchet* tells the story of a boy who survives the crash of a small airplane, only to find himself marooned in a vast wilderness with nothing at hand but his wits and a hatchet. How many times had Penny and I read that book aloud, our sons tucked against us, rapt at the words they'd heard so many times before. And they have always loved books about Native American skills and culture, in which deep reverence for the natural world includes the frequent taking of life.

As soon as they were physically able, they began living out fantasies of survival. When Fin was four, Penny found him in the woods bordering our yard. He'd liberated a dead mouse from a snap trap in the basement and taken it to the forest, where he'd proceeded to skin and gut it. The "pelt" (as he called it) had been hung to dry, alongside a pair of tiny "hams." He'd seen us slaughter and butcher a number of livestock, and therefore had an understanding of the process, but this seemed like something more than simple emulation.

"How did he even know how to do that?" I asked.

Penny just shrugged her shoulders. "I think it's just *in* him," she said.

Still, none of this prepared us for the reality of our children on the land, traps and weapons in hand. None of it prepared us for the possibility of examining our own feelings about such practices. Once again, our children were forcing us to learn and unlearn, to reach outside our comfort zone. Penny discussed this with the boys' mentor, Erik, a man they held in the highest regard. We assumed he'd recoil at the notion of our sons' trapping, at which point we could put the whole sordid affair to rest, once and for all.

Alas, that was not exactly how it played out. "Actually, some people consider trapping more humane than hunting, because it reduces the chances of an animal being wounded and escaping," he told her. Furthermore, he informed her, he had a friend who was an avid trapper, a man who'd learned from the Cree Indians of Northern Quebec. This man did not trap for profit. He trapped only when he had a specific use for the animal in mind, and he utilized every feasible part of the creatures he killed. He ate muskrat and made knife sheaths from beaver tails. He was in the process of sewing a beaver-pelt vest. He was gentle and thoughtful, and he believed, as the Cree do, that trapping these animals was to enter into relationship with them. He believed, in a way that was not immediately obvious to Penny and me, that trapping these animals brought him closer to them.

And that's how we met Nate, who, through a series of serendipitous circumstances, came to live with us. He'd needed to move out of the house where he was staying, and we had just recently constructed a small, rustic outbuilding, originally intended to serve as a "milking room," but which stood empty. The Nate Crate is what the boys dubbed the milking-room-turned-boarding-shack, shortly after he'd arrived in June. He showed up in his pickup truck full of belongings, the majority of which he'd made with his own two hands.

As we soon learned, six years prior, when he was thirty, Nate had up and quit pretty much everything he was doing in order to devote himself to acquiring wilderness skills and building meaningful relationships with the natural world. "I realized I didn't know anything that really mattered," is how he explained it, and I immediately understood what he meant. Like many people, I am often struck by the fact that the modern world is full of affected knowledge and information that, when you get right down to it, is only relevant to the extent we grant it relevance. We have become very good at procuring and prioritizing things that are not fundamentally all that important—cars and computers and cell phones come to mind—even as we have become less good at providing for ourselves the things that are downright essential: Food. Shelter. Water. Warmth.

For the past half-dozen years, Nate had been living in tents, cabins, yurts, and snow caves, while immersing himself in a self-directed course of study for all the things you don't learn in school. He had made snowshoes, a toboggan, and numerous articles of clothing, generally from the coats and skins of wild animals he had trapped or shot. He was in the process of building a birchbark canoe, and played a mean fiddle. He did not spend much money, and seemed quite content to not know where he'd be living come winter. It wouldn't be in the Nate Crate, that much was clear from the way the wind whistled through the gaping cracks between the siding boards.

One night shortly after he arrived, a massive thunderstorm

blew in. The sky went all dusky, and lightning started splashing everywhere, and the wind got furious and gnashing. Penny and I stood on the threshold of the French doors that open from our kitchen onto a small stone patio, watching the storm move across the sky. We could just hear Nate's fiddle riding above the clamor of it all; he was down in his little cabin, sitting in the gathering dark, playing to the storm. Penny and I stood there even as the rain began pelting down so hard it actually hurt, watching the trees writhe in the wind and listening to the music carrying up from Nate's fiddle, and I realized that what inspired me about Nate was not so much the specific skills he had learned but the simple fact that he had taken his life into his own hands. It takes courage to do such a thing, to conduct oneself in accordance with beliefs that do not enjoy widespread support, and his presence became a living reminder that we are often freer than we might otherwise believe.

The boys, of course, were ecstatic to have Nate around, as it meant they had a live-in teacher for all the things they dreamed of knowing. Shortly after arriving at our place, Nate began helping Fin and Rye construct a pair of shaving horses, starting with a length of birch they split with wedges. He loaned the boys each a drawknife, and for a week or so, their spare moments were consumed by carving and shaping. He took the boys turkey hunting. They went fishing. They disappeared into the woods to follow animal trails visible only to the trained eye.

In this manner, the story of Fin and Rye's trapping and hunting is not merely the story of their trapping and hunting. Indeed, it is the story of many of the aspects crucial to how they learn and develop. It is the story of mentors, of people like Nate, who have taken an interest in our sons and whose generosity with their time and knowledge cannot be overstated. The role of mentors in our culture seems to have been reduced to programs intended for youth "in need," those unfortunate children whose parents are not fully able to embody healthy, stable role modeling. But of course all children are *in need* to a certain extent. As present, attentive, and well meaning as Penny and I are, Fin and Rye were in need of someone to guide them through the skills and ethics of trapping. They needed someone to validate their interests and instincts, someone whose words carried the authority of experience and respect. Because let's face it: children don't always consider their parents to be fonts of wisdom, and it was not long before the phrase "Nate says" became a common refrain in our home.

Mentors are disappearing across the landscape of contemporary childhood learning and development. And how could it be otherwise? Because how many adults even have time to mentor anymore? Furthermore, after school and after-school activities, and after homework, television, and texting, how many children even have time to be mentored?

But my sons' foray into hunting and trapping is about more than mentoring, because it has reminded me once again that when they are granted the freedom to follow their passion, they learn quickly. I almost wrote "effortlessly," but that's not true. Their learning isn't effortless; it merely appears that way, because they do not struggle against it. Penny and I watched in amazement as they studied for hours at a time in order to pass the safety certification courses necessary to earn their hunting and trapping licenses. For weeks on end, they bent over the state-supplied workbooks, writing their answers in the careful, blocky penmanship common to youth. "Look at them," said Penny one day, as they sat across the table from one another, immersed in their respective workbooks. "They're learning how to memorize useless information in order to pass a test, just like in school!"

Indeed, much of the information in the books *was* fairly useless, at least for two boys who already knew they should dress in layers on cold days and never look down the barrel of a loaded gun. But of course their immersion into hunting and trapping, facilitated by Nate, has also taught them many things that are of tremendous and enduring value.

Not long after they passed their respective tests and were granted their licenses, Penny and I brainstormed a list of all the subjects their interest in trapping had exposed them to. It was merely out of curiosity, because by this point in their unschooled education, we were confident our sons were learning everything they truly needed to know. We felt no need to categorize their learning into respective subjects, in part because we had long ago come to understand that such categorization was an affectation. Still, it was fascinating to see how Fin and Rye's self-directed learning could be understood and explained in the common terminology of modern education, as well as the so-called "soft skills" of human socialization and self-regulation.

Here's the list we came up with:

- Money Management—saving for supplies, evaluating purchases and the value of these purchases
- Math—primarily in the context of money management, but also in consideration of the land's capacity to support a given number of animals
- Time Management—how to structure their days to accommodate running the trapline and other commitments, such as chores
- Biology and Earth Sciences—study of the habitats and habits of their quarry, how weather and climate impacts wildlife, reproductive cycles, and so on
- Anatomy—identification of internal organs and other aspects of physical anatomy via skinning, dressing, butchering
- Physical Education—as evidenced by their endless forays over hill and dale, shouldering thirty-pound packs
- Ethics—the importance of using all parts of animals, giving thanks, not trapping more than they can actually use/consume, utilizing traps designed to minimize pain
- Teamwork—negotiating whose traps would be set where, how to best lay out trapline to meet expectations of time management, interdependence/cooperation
- Geography—consulting both tax and topographic maps to determine who owns the land they wish to hunt and trap, and also to determine how best to design their trapline

- Reading and Writing—the completion of their hunting and trapping workbooks, the actual tests, and the numerous letters to landowners seeking permission to trap on their land, which provided ample opportunity to hone their reading and writing, including spelling, penmanship, sentence and paragraph formation, and their general ability to communicate effectively via the written word
- Human Relations—knocking on doors during the quest to secure hunting and trapping permission and remaining positive and friendly even in the face of frequent refusals

This list could continue, I suspect. But the truth is, while I recognize the value of these subjects and whatever ones could be added, there is something about defining and isolating them that profoundly misses the point. Because in doing so, each subject becomes segregated from the others in a way that exists only in the vacuum of structured learning. Such segregation is not the way of the natural world, where all of these aspects form an ecosystem of knowledge and experience that cannot be defined by the commonplace vernacular of standardized learning. This is precisely why so much of the learning that happens in schools feels irrelevant beyond the classroom.

Still, I cannot deny gleaning a certain satisfaction and perhaps even comfort from this list, if only because already it has helped me explain my children's education in a manner that is broadly understood. Yes, I do believe it is flawed to think of learning in such overly simplistic terms, but that is nonetheless how most people have come to think of it, and there is not always time to engage in a more meaningful discussion. In a sense, the list that Penny and I came up with provides a convenient bridge between our sons' atypical education and the prevailing educational orthodoxy, flawed as it might be.

Finally, while Penny and I are fortunate that our parents and extended family generally support our choices around education, not all parents who walk an atypical path are so lucky. Therefore, I humbly offer this thought experiment in the hope that it might help these parents demonstrate their children's learning in the context of convention.

Nate eventually moved from the Nate Crate, chased by the cold winds of autumn into the insulated protection of a yurt he'd constructed from scratch. A few weeks later, he sent a letter to the boys. It was a long letter, four pages in all, single spaced and written in his careful hand. Reading it to the boys, I realized how incredibly blessed we are. To have Nate in our lives, yes, but also to have structured our lives in such a manner that our lives could accommodate Nate in the first place. To have been able to allow our sons the freedom to learn from him, to spend long hours sitting in the Crate or just outside it, bent over some task or another, or to pass the day walking the woods with him, or in a canoe, making their way down a sinuous river. To have allowed ourselves the freedom to unlearn so much of what we thought we knew, not only about hunting and trapping but also about what learning can be, and who should teach us.

Is a beaver just another piece of skin to be stripped and sold, or is he an animal with his own life and part in creation, an orange-toothed fat-bellied dark-haired night swimmer who knows worlds we can't imagine, experiences life in ways we'll never know, and deserves his place on Earth as much as anyone or anything?

You two will have to find your own way in this. How to make your living in such a way that it fits with your beliefs. The more you know, the more options you have, and the more freedom you have to live outside convention, if this is what you choose . . . the easiest thing to do is what everyone else is doing.

Our first task is to treat each other well, for when we learn to always offer respect, kindness, and generosity to those around us, it spreads outward into our relationship with the rest of the world, and the Earth opens up to us in ways we never imagined.

What has Nate taught Fin and Rye? Geography, anatomy, biology, yes. Some history, ethics, a bit of science, absolutely. How to pound a length of brown ash into splits for weaving into baskets. How to scrape and stretch a freshly slaughtered steerhide so it will dry properly, and then how to make it into sandals. Much like the list of subjects Penny and I came up with, this one could go on. And on.

But I'm pretty sure the boys are learning something more from their friend, too. It defies ready explanation, perhaps because it does not fit within the catalog of segregated subjects that defines most institutional learning. There is no class in this lesson, and there is no way to grade one's progress. The learning required will never be finished. Yet it's probably the most important thing my sons will ever learn.

It is an understanding of their place in the grand scheme of this big and imperfect world. It is their recognition of the need to ask questions of themselves and of others, and the knowledge that the answers they get should not always be taken at face value. They are learning to consider how everything they do affects everything else, and they are learning that there are worlds where orange-toothed fat-bellied dark-haired night swimmers move in shadows beneath the water.

Will Fin and Rye ever fully know these worlds? No. But they're learning something else, too: sometimes it's OK to *not* know.

THE FREEDOM TO LEARN

It was twelve-below this morning, an even dozen degrees to the underside of zero, and I couldn't quite get the image of a full carton of eggs out of my mind, each egg a frigid digit, freezing my appendages, one at a time. Ridiculous, I know, but there you have it. In any case, it was the coldest it'd been in a good long while, although apparently not cold enough to keep Penny from opening the bedroom window before we turned in for the night. I'm generally grateful to be married to a woman who insists on sleeping beneath an open window 365 nights per year, but I can't quite stop thinking about all those waves of hard-earned heat radiating off the woodstove, only to funnel out that two-inch gap and into the frigid expanse. But damned if I don't know when to pick a battle and when to simply burrow deeper into the covers.

During the summer and fall Penny milks, but in winter, when it comes to feel like something that approaches a chore, we split milking duties, alternating days. Today was mine. I waited until seven forty or so, knowing that at about seven forty-five, the first slanting rays of sun would pop over the small rise to the immediate east of the barn's opening, basking the milking stanchion in their honeyed glow. Cold or no, there is nothing better than milking in the morning's first sun. The warming rays release the soft smells of hay and cow, and when my fingers start stinging from the cold, I ball them up, tuck them into my jacket pockets, and turn my face into the sun as it rises another inch over the horizon.

As I milked, I could hear the boys down in the woods, already deep into some game of imagination or another, and I had to grin. Twelve below zero and my children were playing in the woods. It occurred to me, and not for the first time, that they have much to teach me. And how much they have already taught me. How to harvest stinging wood nettles without getting stung. ("You need to pick them like this, Papa," Rye says, and I bend low so he can demonstrate.) Where the fiddlehead ferns grow. How to build a water-tight shelter of sticks and leaves, and a fire with flint and steel. The difference between thinking cold and feeling cold. That fox pee smells like skunk. ("Sniff," says Fin, crouched over a yellow divot in the snow, and so I drop to my knees to smell fox piss with my son. He's right, of course. It smells just like skunk.)

They have taught me nature is full of more small wonders than I will ever know, and even that not knowing is OK, too.

They have taught me patience. So, so much patience.

How many of these things would I have learned if Penny and I had sent them out of our lives for eight or more hours each day? How many would I have learned if I'd sent myself out of their lives for eight or more hours each day, if we had not chosen to commit ourselves to this piece of land, to this way of life? We do not allow our children to learn at home simply so we can learn from them. Such a thing would be selfish. But in allowing them the freedom to learn as they grow, an unanticipated and beautiful thing has happened: We have allowed ourselves the same freedom.

11

How It Ends

I WISH I COULD TELL YOU how all of this ends. I wish I could report that Fin and Rye have grown into young men who are finding their way in a world that is evolving toward the most beautiful expression of what the world can be. I wish I could say with certainty that my children have made their place in this community, or in another community; that they have fallen in love, or have not; that they have had children, or have not. I wish I could tell you that my sons' atypical education has impacted them in ways that are only positive, that they have never been denied an opportunity because of their unconventional childhood. It would be meaningful for me to offer evidence that their relationship to the natural world has continued into adulthood and has somehow informed their lives for the better.

Furthermore, I would like to write that Penny and I have aged with grace, right here on this same small piece of ground, sheltered by the same slanting roof under which Fin and Rye took their first breaths. If I could, I would say that we have never regretted any of our choices—those made both for ourselves and on behalf of the boys—and that our faith in what it means to be whole and happy has never been broken. I have this image in my head—dangerous, I know—of the two of us, slower, less steady, stooped, our bodies inevitably giving way to gravity's demands, still going about our days much the same as we do now. In the morning start the fire, feed the cows, and slop the pigs; then breakfast and work. In the afternoon, a project, wood to be split, or something to be repaired or built, friends visiting or visited. Chores again and dinner. Reading. Bed. Sleep.

I want to write that some of those who have been most meaningful to us have moved on—our parents, Melvin, Martha—and that their departure has made room for others to move into our lives. It would be nice to say that although we still do not have much money, we never want for more; that most of our needs remain simple, and that all of our needs, those simple and those complex, are met. I want to tell you that on clear, moonlit nights in winter we still ski what was once Melvin's hayfield, and I still watch the moon climb into the sky. I still feel impermanence and connectivity. I still feel wonder. I still feel held.

If I could write the end of this book from that unknown place in the future, I would hope that the clarity of my beliefs regarding what is possible remains unclouded. I would hope that I could look back over my life and see that I had acted on those beliefs, even as the story of our time suggested I was foolish for having done so. I would hope that I hadn't succumbed to cynicism, but instead had remained earnest, honest, grateful, and perhaps even naive in my dealings and interpretations of the world around me. I would hope that this would no longer feel like something to strive for, but rather something I had long ago attained.

There are times when I wonder if we have it all backward. And I wonder how the world might be if we viewed the very reason for our existence as being not about control and security but about surrender. Not to our fears and insecurities but to our sense of what is possible, to the belief that we all have the ability to shape the world as we imagine it, and that our actions reflect this imagined world until it becomes not imagined, but real. What if we understood— what if we felt we could *afford* to understand—that whatever harm we do the natural world, we do to ourselves? That whatever harm we do to others, we do to ourselves? What if we did not worry about being taken advantage of by immigrants, by minorities, by corporations, by politicians, by government? What if we no longer worried that others might perceive us as naive? What if the point were not to know as much as possible but to *feel* as much as possible? What if every day, come sun, rain, snow, heat, or cold, we pledged to find a tree, small or tall, straight or curved, leafed or not, and we sat with our back against its trunk for no less than a dozen minutes? What if we thought we could feel the tree breathing? What if we actually could?

And finally: what if we taught our children accordingly?

Of course, to do so does not require that we unschool or homeschool our children. Nor is it incompatible with much of the rote information that now comprises the majority of institutionalized learning, some of which is enormously helpful, and even essential. Addition, subtraction, writing, reading: all of these and more are necessary for a child—not to mention an adult—to communicate with his family and community. But the truth is that they can be learned with surprisingly little effort, and in a surprisingly scant amount of time, and always in the context of a child's true interests and passions.

In truth, we have spent almost *no* time teaching this information to Fin and Rye; indeed, we have found that they learn and retain it best when they are allowed to do so at their own behest. We did not teach Fin how to read, but instead read to him and around him, and one day it happened that our son noticed whenever we skipped a word or passage. Not many days later, he began picking up books and reading to himself. Rye has come to reading more slowly, but in much the same way. "Mama, you missed a word," he'll say as Penny reads, because, of course, he's been reading right along with her.

The math they need is all around us, even in our fields and gardens. "How much garlic do I need to save for next year's seed?" Fin asks us, and the calculations begin: There are five cloves per bulb, and he needs to plant a bulb every six inches along a forty-five-foot strip of soil. He scrunches his face like any child would, chasing the answer in his head. Fin has been slower to math than his brother;

he is in general not as precise a child as Rye and more content with something being "close enough." But as he matures, he is realizing that precision has its place. Not long ago, after years of steadfast denials that math was even a necessary skill, he said to Penny, "OK, Mama, I have to get better with math." And he has. Not because we've forced him to but because he wants to. Because he recognized that he needed to.

Fin and Rye have learned to write the way all children learn to write: by writing. But rather than demand that they spend hours practicing penmanship, the boys have learned to write as a natural extension of their desire to send letters to family and friends. They have kept on-and-off-again journals of their adventures or in order to track their goats' breeding schedules. They love to draw cartoons, full of thought bubbles and bawdy conversations.

Having witnessed, time and again, my sons' ability to quickly learn the essential skills of modern life in the context of their interests, I am struck by just how much of our children's time we waste on rote learning in isolation from other knowledge and experience. Even as I write these words, I can feel the frustration and even anger I knew as a teen, the sense of my time being stolen from me just so I could meet someone else's expectations of how and what I should learn. I am struck by how disrespectful this is to children, and how it cannot help but teach them that their lives are not their own. Yes, there is more to a schooled education than reading, writing, and arithmetic, but like most adults I know, I struggle to recall precisely what I learned in school, and I strongly believe this is because it was learned in isolation from anything that mattered to me. It was learned solely because I was told it must be learned and because I passed my days learning what I was told must be learned, I was not free to pursue my own passions. Or even develop them in the first place.

Does our self-directed approach sometimes mean that my boys do not "perform" to the standards set by contemporary educational assumptions? As a matter of fact, it does. For instance, Fin did not learn to read until he was nearly eight, and Rye seems to be tracking nearly a year behind him. Quite clearly, there are things that many of their peers know—some of whom attend school, some of whom don't—that my boys don't know. Some of these things they will learn as they need to learn them; some they may not ever learn. Do not think that just because your child is unschooled he will self-direct himself to memorize every capitol city of every state, or the date of every important historical event. But I have seen that if I can let go of my fear and simply trust them, they will learn what they need to learn, and they will do it happily, without anger or the sense that their destiny is not their own. It is not that I wish to protect my sons from all the emotions learning gives rise to. I know they will frequently be frustrated. I know that often they will fail. But frustration and failure are as natural, healthy, and essential to their development as confidence, success, and joy.

Of course there is knowledge and experience contained in the vessels of my young sons that eludes the vast majority of their peers. That eludes the vast majority of adults, even. I see the way they move through the forest, stopping to pluck a handful of wood sorrel or chanterelle mushrooms, or to point out the scratch marks of a wild turkey or, in the winter, the oval of a deer's bed. Everywhere, I see the evidence of their knowledge and learning. The multitudinous structures they've built, some of evident purpose and careful design and some that appear purposeless. Or the pack baskets they use almost every day; they're only a year old, and already they are ragged at the edges, the thin splints of wood fraying like fabric. Or the wool hats they felted the day after our sheep were shorn.

You might ask, "What is the point of knowing these things?" To which I can only answer, "What is the point of knowing anything?" By extension, we might both ask, "What is the point of an education?" Is it to be socialized to a particular set of expectations? Is it to continue sawing at the few frayed strands still connecting us to the natural world? Is it to learn that learning happens best under the gaze of a specialist? If so, then perhaps you are correct. There is no point to my sons knowing what fox pee smells like, or which of the wild mushrooms in our forest are edible, or how to make fire from sticks. There is no point to the ease and comfort with which they move through the wilderness. There is no point to their desire to help our neighbor get his hay under cover before the rain comes. There is no point to their boundless curiosity regarding the habits of the woodland animals. There is no point to all the little shelters and tools they've built.

But what if, as I suggested at the outset of this book, the point of a child's education simply cannot be found or measured in the context of performance-based assessments, standardized tests, or projected lifetime income? What if the point of an education is to imbue our children with a sense of their connectivity, not merely with other humans but also with the trees and animals and soil and moon and sky? What if the point of *life* is to feel these connections, and all the emotions they give rise to?

What then?

I am often asked what might happen to our society if every child were educated in the manner of Fin and Rye. What if every child was granted the freedom to learn at his or her own pace, according to his or her specific interests? What of the many highly trained professionals upon which we all rely, the doctors, surgeons, engineers, pilots, and so many more? Where would they come from? How would they learn the incredibly important and specific knowledge their trades demand? Surely not by knowing how to craft a long bow. Certainly not by spending their days in the forest, or bent over a pot of boiling sap, their cheeks moist with steam, their hair absorbing the acrid smell of wood smoke.

But such questions—while certainly logical—are inherently flawed, because they assume that a childhood of self-directed learning is incompatible with the higher education the aforementioned careers require. Likewise, we seem to be afflicted by a cultural belief that if you don't compel people to learn, they will choose not to learn. This belief is rooted in the fallacy that people are inherently lazy and disinterested. It is rooted in the misconception that a child can choose to *not* learn.

Indeed, I have found that the truth is exactly the opposite. When you allow people—both children and adults—the freedom to learn what they want, when they want, they come to their learning with fierce passion and energy. They come to it not because they are motivated to make money but because they are driven by something far more powerful than material gain: love of knowledge and the very process of attaining knowledge. The result is that they end up learning and doing what they *should* be learning and doing, when they should be learning and doing it, and for this simple reason they become better at whatever occupation they have chosen, whether it is farmer, lawyer, doctor, mechanic, carpenter, artist, logger, and even teacher. And the world becomes better for it.

Of course, not every child—no matter the structure (or lack thereof) of their education—will turn to the land in the manner of my sons. And while I am deeply grateful for my children's connection to nature and to the place we live, I have seen how other families, under vastly different circumstances, have also benefited from loosening their grip over their children's education and time. I know of unschooled children in cities who are thriving and finding meaning and purpose in their days, just as I know of unschooled children in the country who do not make bows and maple syrup but are nonetheless blossoming in the context of their own self-directed passions. Unschooling is not about the discovery of any particular body of knowledge. It is about the discovery of *self*.

Am I really advocating for an end to school? I am not, although at times it must seem as if I am. But in truth it hardly matters. Such a thing as ending institutionalized learning is unrealistic, anyway. It has been less than a century since every state in the union adopted compulsory schooling, but in that time our society has become utterly dependent on school, in no small part because we inhabit an economy that grants few of us the freedom to allow our children to follow a different path. The difficult truth is that even for families that might otherwise choose to educate at home, school performs the crucial function of giving their children somewhere to go while parents work the jobs necessary to make ends meet. It's not that public education is particularly affordable (in fact, it is precisely the opposite), but few families can afford to consider alternatives.

What's more, we have become emotionally dependent on school. After so many decades of being socialized to the notion that a child's learning must be structured, measured, and mandated, we find it nearly impossible to believe otherwise. It is not our fault, because most of us were "taught" in precisely this manner. In the process, our innate love of learning was wounded, and our connections to nature and the community and world beyond the classroom became frayed. They are not severed, because they can never truly be severed—they exist whether we care to acknowledge them or not. But by not acknowledging them, by not reveling in them, we cannot achieve our full potential as human beings.

Penny and I have had to unlearn so much. Indeed, we are still unlearning, and will be until the day we die. In a very real sense, it is not our sons who needed unschooling: it is us. Our sons' unschooling has become our unschooling, and the freedom we have granted them to embrace learning is a freedom we have granted ourselves. Fin and Rye are teaching us so much, not merely the small specifics of this time and place but also the lessons that no curriculum, no matter how rigorous or comprehensive, can teach. How to find one's place in a world that can occasionally seem inhospitable. How and where to find beauty and contentment in the minutia of our days. What can be let go of and what should be retained.

There is a place for school in these lessons, but it is not the place most schooling currently occupies. Still, there are models of how a school can become an institution that does not stifle the human desire to learn but instead supports and facilitates it. There are places like the Sudbury Valley School, in Framingham, Massachusetts, where children are allowed to learn at their own pace, and in the manner of their choosing. The Sudbury Valley School follows a model created by Britain's Summerhill School, in which adults are on hand to facilitate and advise, but never to mandate and, via the accepted norms of grades, recognition, and advancement, demean. In fact, at both Summerhill and Sudbury, founded in 1921 and 1968, respectively, students can even vote whether or not to renew a teacher's contract.

It was never my intention for this book to be prescriptive in nature, but rather to share my family's journey and some of the stories we've collected along our path toward rooting ourselves into this small piece of land. The constellation of decisions surrounding this rooting—to unschool our children, to pass our days in the quiet, settled manner necessitated by the seasonal rituals inherent in a small farm, to create a life that might be seen by some as needlessly simple or even lacking—has enriched our lives in ways that seem to never stop surprising me. It is as if one discovery leads to another, one lesson heralding the next, and I cannot overstate the extent to which my sons open the door to these lessons. My gratitude to them, and to Penny, who works so hard to facilitate their self-directed learning, is profound.

Like most people I know, I experience moments of uncertainty about choices I have made. There are so many permutations of what it means to live a good life. There are so many ways to be. *How can I ever choose between them all?* But then summer comes, and I'm riding the hay wagon behind Martha, and I'm dripping sweat and my arms shake as I pass another bale back to Penny and the boys, and I feel the quiet comfort of knowing there is nothing else I want or need.

And I feel like this when I'm moving the cows to a fresh paddock and it's early and the sun is just coming up and my feet are wet from dew and I'm moving fast because I'm shivering a little. And the cows, they know exactly what I'm doing because we do this dance every damn day and they stand at the fence watching my every move, waiting for the moment I drop the wire. I feel like this when I'm standing in Melvin's barnyard and we're talking cows or politics or machinery or weather or he's telling me about the heifer that was born the day before and she almost didn't make it but she did and I should really see the mark on her forehead, it looks just like a little bird.

And I feel like this when I catch a glimpse of Fin and Rye moving along the forest's edge, on their way to some adventure I will never be fully privy to, exploring some world that is not mine to know. In these moments, I see how they are becoming more self-contained, and I feel the passing ache of the knowledge that someday, they will leave this place. It may seem as if this is far in the future, but I know that when it happens, I will look back over the intervening years and realize that it was merely a sliver of time, a window that has closed but which, through recalling, invites my gaze.

Epilogue: Moonstruck

After evening chores, the four of us strap on our skis. It is late December and a minor storm has moved through. Three inches, or maybe even less. That morning, I'd told the boys I didn't think there was enough snow for skiing. "Doesn't look very good," I said dismissively. "Bony."

They'd ignored me and skied anyway, hour after hour up and down the big hill in our pasture, falling and laughing and arguing about where to go next and how to build the jump. I watched them through the warm side of my office window, and not for the first time I realized how much my sons have to teach me and how quiet those lessons can be. So quiet I could miss them. "Doesn't look very good," I'd said. "Bony," I'd said. Well, it was sure as heck good enough for them.

The boys were right. The skiing is excellent, the snow fast and yielding, the air cold but not too cold. The four of us glide out onto Melvin's hayfield, its frozen surface shorn by his cows' autumn grazing. Blood rushes to my cheeks. I can feel it there, puddled and warm.

The idea had been to ski under the nearly full moon; the full moon had risen two nights prior, but two nights prior the ground had been bereft of snow. Tonight, for the first half hour or so, we skied in the inky darkness, and the sky was an unbroken blanket of blue black, as if a curtain had been drawn over the cosmos. "Where's the moon, Papa?" Rye asked, and I explained that soon it would rise and our way would be lighted as surely as if the sun itself had broken over the horizon. "You wait and see," I said. "It's going to be something."

We skied on. But after another twenty minutes, it was still dark, and the boys were getting antsy, and I began to wonder if I'd somehow gotten confused, if perhaps the idea of a waning moon is a myth and the lunar cycle actually goes from full start to full stop in just one day, a light switch that can be turned on and off.

Finally, with my confidence in my grasp of the lunar rhythms at an all-time low, a soft glow emerged from behind the northeastern horizon, as if a light were shining in the depths of dark water. "Here it comes," I said, but the boys seemed skeptical. The preceding half hour had dented my credibility. But soon the glow brightened and then, inch by inch, the moon began to rise. We stopped and watched, and even the boys—especially the boys—were transfixed. We could actually see it rising, could track its progress through the sky. It was as if the moon had been catapulted from somewhere deep in the earth's core, as if it had finally broken free of binding chains, and within minutes, the entire landscape was brushed in a warm, almost intoxicating glow. For a moment I experienced a feeling that was not immediately familiar, but which I soon came to identify as the sensation of being comforted.

I glanced at the boys, their faces awash in the soft light. I'd thought that perhaps I might try to articulate what I was feeling, and wondered if they'd understand even if I could express it. But seeing them standing there, mesmerized by the scene unfolding before them, I had to chuckle at my naïveté. I didn't need to say a word. My children understood better than I ever would.

At Thanksgiving, only a few weeks prior, a friend of ours had told me that humans are able to perceive only 1 percent of what's out there. In other words, there are another 99 percent of sights and sounds, smells, tastes, and textures that we know nothing about. I was not sure how she knew this or if I should even believe it. But just as I cannot know it to be true, I cannot know it to be untrue.

If there really is another 99 percent of experience I will never understand, there is much I cannot know. More than I ever before realized.

Here, then, is the antidote to the flawed hypothesis of human exceptionalism: a moon, white and bright and pushing through the ether so fast that its movement is actually discernible on a moment-by-moment basis, a soaring bird etched against a wedge of sky. Two children ages nine and seven, heads tilted toward the sky, faces half-lit by the strange, milky light cast from above, enthralled. A rolling field, all hummock and sag, stretching in all directions toward its borders, ill defined in the soft luminescence. And beneath it all a gathering, almost viral sensation of insignificance, the awareness that everything my senses tell me to be true might be only a fraction of all there is to know.

For fifteen minutes or so, we watched and then, cold and hungry, we skied home. I stoked the fire and we ate.

Note to the Reader

I did not want this book to be overtly prescriptive. Partly this is because so many aspects of how my children learn and live are dependent on circumstances unique to our family. But it's also because the choices all parents make about their children's education are incredibly personal. Finally, not everyone who reads this book is willing to relinquish certain expectations for their children's learning.

Still, anyone who's read this far may be curious about granting their children the freedom to self-direct a portion of their learning. Perhaps in the process, they will be encouraged to reconnect with their natural surroundings. With these parents in mind I offer the following ideas for starting this process, even in the context of a more conventional educational path. Because it is difficult to liberate one's children without liberating oneself first, some of these ideas are geared toward adults, too.

Play hooky.

If you have school-aged children, take them out of school for a day. Take the day off work yourself. Unplug every screen in your house. For at least part of the day, go with your children to the woods, or to a park, or to the middle of a hayfield. Have no agenda, bring no toys or games. Lie on your backs, or lean against a tree. Close your eyes. Open them. Talk. Be silent. Smell. Hear. *Be.*

Turn off the news.

Turn off the Internet news, the television news, the radio news, and the print news. Turn it all off. Do this because there is nothing in the news—no matter how tragic or unsettling it may be—that truly matters in the *here* and *now* of your life. Do this because any emotional energy you expend fretting about news that doesn't truly matter in the here and now of your life is not energy you have to expend on the things that actually do matter.

Stay home.

Cancel nonessential plans or, better yet, don't make those plans to begin with. Don't stay home forever, but do stay home long enough that leaving home feels like something to appreciate and savor, not just something that makes your life more complicated, and not just something you do because you never considered *not* doing it.

Make something with your child.

It does not have to be complicated, but it should serve a specific function, and its making should necessitate the use of tools that require skill and good judgment to handle safely. You might build a catapult from scrap lumber, or carve a spoon from a tree branch. You might construct a weather-tight shelter or a tree house. And when you are finished making whatever it is you make, *use it.*

Grow something with your child.

Organic vegetable grower Eliot Coleman told me once, "It's important for democracy to have a certain percentage of people feeding themselves so they can tell government to go f**k off." So grow something. I'm tempted to say "grow anything," but frankly, there's already enough zucchini in the world. So, anything but zucchini, OK?

Go outside. Stay outside.

Some early morning very soon, walk outside, close your eyes, tilt your face to the sky, and stay that way for at least one minute. If it's sunny, feel the sun. If it's raining, feel the rain. If it's cold, feel the cold. If you are uncomfortable, be uncomfortable. It's only for a minute. You'll be OK.

Sleep outdoors.

Not in a tent, but in the open air, so that when you awake you're damp with morning dew and just a bit chilly. Helpful hint: Wait until autumn, when the mosquitos have beaten their annual retreat. Because it's one thing to wake up a little wet and cold; it's entirely another to be kept up all night by ruthless pests.

Step away from your children's play.

Allow them to play with no expectation of learning or results, and furthermore allow them to make their own rules (even if the rules make no sense), to have their own arguments (even if the arguments are loud and silly), and to find their own path toward reconciliation (even if the path is long).

Equip your children to be of use.

Find ways for your children to help around the house. This applies even when their helping isn't helpful. Let them work with you in the garden, even if they pull the carrots before they are ready. Allow them to help you clean the house, even if it the house ends up messier than when you started. Humble yourself to the reality that you will not be as productive as you'd like, but remember that some of what you're producing is a child with confidence, skills, and resourcefulness. A child with these qualities cannot help but share them with others, and that's worth a whole lot more than a few carrots or a clean house.

Trust more.

Remember that children cannot be expected to be responsible if they are not granted responsibility first. They cannot be expected to be trustworthy if we do not show them they are worthy of our trust. These correlations are perfectly logical, but the logic has been lost in an institutionalized educational system that lacks the necessary resources to grant meaningful responsibility and trust to our children.

Make choice matter.

Think of yourself as not merely faced with decisions to which you must react, but as being proactively *at choice*. And when a decision is difficult, consider what you are agreeing to with each choice, and what it says about the world you wish to inhabit.

Do not fear conforming.

Sometimes, conforming is exactly the right thing to do. On the other hand, do be afraid of conforming without realizing you are doing just that.

Notes

Chapter 1. The Reckoning

1. John Holt, *Growing Without Schooling*, no. 2 (1977).

Chapter 4. Drive

1. Peter Gray, *Free to Learn: Why Unleashing the Instinct to Play Will Make Our Children Happier, More Self-Reliant, and Better Students for Life* (New York: Basic Books, 2013).

Chapter 5. The Early Years

1. "F.D.A. Finds Short Supply of Attention Deficit Drugs," *New York Times*, January 1, 2012.
2. Homeschool Legal Defense Association, *Progress Report 2009: Homeschool Academic Achievement and Demographics*, 2009.
3. Andrew Sum, Ishwar Khatiwada, Joseph McLaughlin, with Sheila Palmer, "The Consequences of Dropping Out of High School: Joblessness and Jailing for High School Dropouts and the High Cost for Taxpayers," Center for Labor Market Studies, Northeastern University, Boston, Massachusetts, 2009. www.northeastern.edu/clms/wp-content/uploads/The_Consquences_of_Dropping_Out_of_High_School.pdf.

Chapter 7. The Downside of Convenience

1. Gray, Peter. *Free to Learn: Why Unleashing the Instinct to Play Will Make Our Children Happier, More Self-Reliant, and Better Students for Life* (New York: Basic Books. 2013), p. 218.

Chapter 9. Hay and Responsibility

1. Liedloff, Jean, *The Continuum Concept: In Search of Happiness Lost* (Cambridge, MA: Perseus Books, 1975), p. 103.

Ben Hewitt is the author of *Saved, The Town That Food Saved, Making Supper Safe,* and articles for magazines such as *Bicycling, Discover, Gourmet, Men's Journal, National Geographic Adventure, Outside,* the *New York Times Magazine, Yankee, Taproot,* and many others. He and his family live in a self-built, solar-powered house in Cabot, Vermont, and operate a forty-acre livestock, vegetable, and berry farm. To learn more, visit www.benhewitt.net.